▲▲▲▲▲▲▲▲▲

LITERACY
IN
LIFESKILLS

BOOK 1

▼▼▼▼▼▼▼▼▼

I 9 N 10 Y

O

K M

F 3

2

D

B A

S J

8

C W

E 5

10

LITERACY IN LIFESKILLS

BOOK 1

Sally Gati

City College of San Francisco

Heinle & Heinle Publishers
A Division of Wadsworth, Inc.
Boston, Massachusetts 02116 U.S.A.

7

4

G

X N

L H

M 2450217

Publisher: Stanley J. Galek
Editorial Director: Christopher Foley
Assistant Editor: Margaret M. Morris
Production Supervisor: Patricia Jalbert
Manufacturing Coordinator: Jerry Christopher
Cover Designer: Brian Sheridan
Illustrations: Progressive Typographers, Inc.
Production Supervision: Progressive Typographers, Inc.

Heinle & Heinle Publishers is a division of Wadsworth, Inc.

Manufactured in the United States of America.

ISBN 0-8384-3846-6 (Book 1)

10 9 8 7 6 5 4 3

Much love and thanks to my ever-helpful husband, Frank
and to my ever-supportive son, David.

Thanks, too, to Mary Kapp and to all
the teachers who, for over ten years,
tested these materials.

To all the students who were the reason and
inspiration for developing **Literacy in Lifeskills**
— a special thank you.

Contents

country
phonics: initial T, F, N, C, S, SP
      final R

F M

T

N

Y

K

B

9

R

4

V

I

5

L

C

W

Z

2

3

P

12

8

S

6

CHAPTER 1

▲▲▲▲▲▲▲▲▲

NUMBERS
1–12
AND
UPPER-CASE
LETTERS

A

O

E

Q

I

J

D

7

10

11

U

X

G

H

1. Listen and repeat.

HI

NUMBERS 1–12 AND UPPER-CASE LETTERS

2. Is this the same?
   Circle the same shape.

YES   NO

3

3. Is this the same?
   Circle the same shape.

YES   NO

NUMBERS 1–12 AND UPPER-CASE LETTERS

4. Is this the same?   YES   NO
   Circle the same number.

1	7	4	10	(1)
2	3	5	2	6
3	2	3	8	5
4	4	1	7	4
5	3	2	5	8
6	9	6	8	0
7	1	4	7	9
8	3	8	5	8
9	0	6	8	9
10	1	0	11	10

5. Copy the number.

1 1

Copy the letters.

O O
N N
E E

Copy the word.

ONE ONE ONE

Copy the number.

2 2 2

Copy the letters.

T T
W W

Copy the word.

TWO TWO TWO

6. Read and copy the letters.

O N W T E O W N E T

7. Read and copy the numbers.

1 2 2 1 2 1 2 1 1 2

8. Listen and repeat.

GOOD-BYE

9. Listen and repeat.

1. GOOD MORNING

2. GOOD AFTERNOON

3. GOOD EVENING

10. Copy the number.

3 3 3

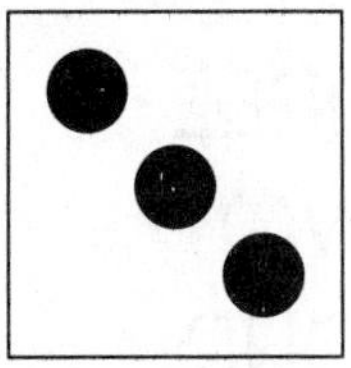

Copy the letters.

H H

R R

Copy the word.

THREE THREE THREE

Copy the number.

4 4 4

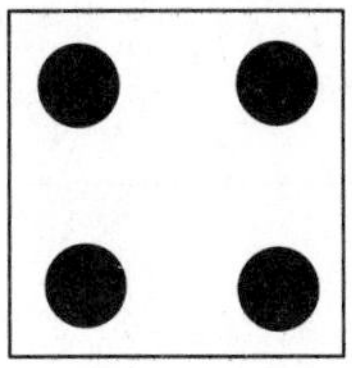

Copy the letters.

F F

U U

Copy the word.

FOUR FOUR FOUR

Copy the number.

5 5 5

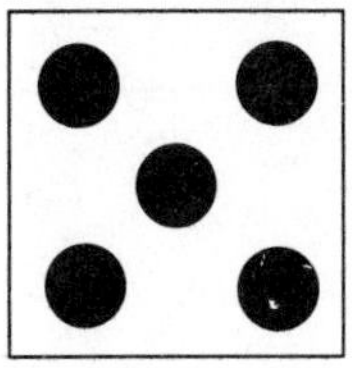

Copy the letters.

I I

V V

Copy the word.

FIVE FIVE FIVE

11. Draw a line to the same number.

2	5		TWO	FIVE
5	3		FIVE	THREE
I	2		ONE	TWO
3	4		THREE	FOUR
4	I		FOUR	ONE

I	THREE		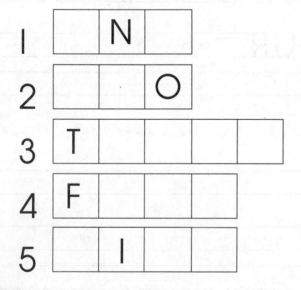	4
5	TWO			5
4	ONE			3
2	FIVE			I
3	FOUR			2

12. Look at the numbers and print the missing letters.

I | | N | |

2 | | | O |

3 | T | | | |

4 | F | | |

5 | | I | | |

13. Print the letters your teacher says (HRFUIV).

1. _____ 2. _____ 3. _____ 4. _____ 5. _____

14. Print the numbers your teacher says (I2345).

1. _____ 2. _____ 3. _____ 4. _____ 5. _____

15. What time is it?
    Read and write the time.

1:00   2:00   3:00   4:00   5:00

1. 1:00

2. 2:00

3. 3:00

4. 4:00

5. 5:00

1. _____

2. _____

3. _____

4. _____

5. _____

16. Count and write the numbers.

| 1 |

△1 △2

①1 ②2 ③3

▽1 ▽2 ▽3 ▽4

◇1 ◇2 ◇3 ◇4 ◇5

_____

_____

_____

_____

_____

_____

_____

_____

_____

_____

_____

_____

_____

_____

_____

_____

1 •
2 • •
3 • • •
4 • • • •
5 • • • • •

ONE

TWO

THREE

FOUR

FIVE

Write the numbers.

3 3 _____

_____

_____

_____

_____

Write the words.

T H R E E

_ _ _ _ _

_ _ _ _ _

_ _ _ _ _

_ _ _ _ _

NUMBERS 1–12 AND UPPER-CASE LETTERS

17.

1	2	3	4	5
ONE	TWO	THREE	FOUR	FIVE

Count the dots.

Write the numbers. ___1___ _____ _____ _____ _____

Print the words. ONE _ _ _ _ _ _ _ _ _ _ _ _ _ _ _

Write the numbers and print the words.

1	_____	3	_____	2
_ _ _	FOUR	_ _ _ _ _	TWO	_ _ _
_____	5	_____	4	_____
THREE	_ _ _ _	ONE	_ _ _ _	FIVE

13

LITERACY IN LIFESKILLS

Print the words.

ONE	_ _ _	_ _ _ _	FOUR	_ _ _ _

_ _ _	TWO	THREE	_ _ _ _	FIVE

Write the numbers.

1	_____	_____	4	_____

_____	2	3	_____	5

_____	_____	_____	_____	_____

Write how many.

_____

_____

_____

_____

_____

14

18. Copy the number.

6 6 6

Copy the letters.

S S

X X

Copy the word.

SIX SIX SIX

Copy the number.

7 7 7

Copy the letters.

V V

N N

Copy the word.

SEVEN SEVEN SEVEN

Copy the number.

8 8 8

Copy the letters.

G G

H H

Copy the word.

EIGHT EIGHT EIGHT

Copy the number.

9   9 9

Copy the word.

NINE   NINE NINE

Copy the number.

10   10 10

Copy the word.

TEN   TEN TEN

STOP

19. Print the letters your teacher says. (SXVNGHOT)

1. ___N___ 2. _____ 3. _____ 4. _____ 5. _____

6. _____ 7. _____ 8. _____ 9. _____ 10. _____

20. Print the numbers your teacher says. (1 2 3 4 5 6 7 8 9 10)

1. ___4___ 2. _____ 3. _____ 4. _____ 5. _____

6. _____ 7. _____ 8. _____ 9. _____ 10. _____

21. Count and write the numbers.

1   2   3   4   5   6   7   8   9   10

ONE TWO THREE FOUR FIVE SIX SEVEN EIGHT NINE TEN

☐ ____1

○○ ____

△△△ ____

◖◖◖ ____

◇◇◇◇ ____

▷▷▷▷▷ ____

◁◁◁◁◁◁ ____

⌒⌒⌒⌒⌒⌒ ____

▯▯▯▯▯▯▯ ____

⌣⌣⌣⌣⌣⌣⌣ ____

Write the numbers.

6 6 6 _____

_____

_____

_____

_____

_____

_____

_____

_____

_____

Write the words.

S I X

_ _ _

_ _ _

_ _ _

_ _ _

_ _ _

_ _ _

_ _ _

_ _ _

_ _ _

17

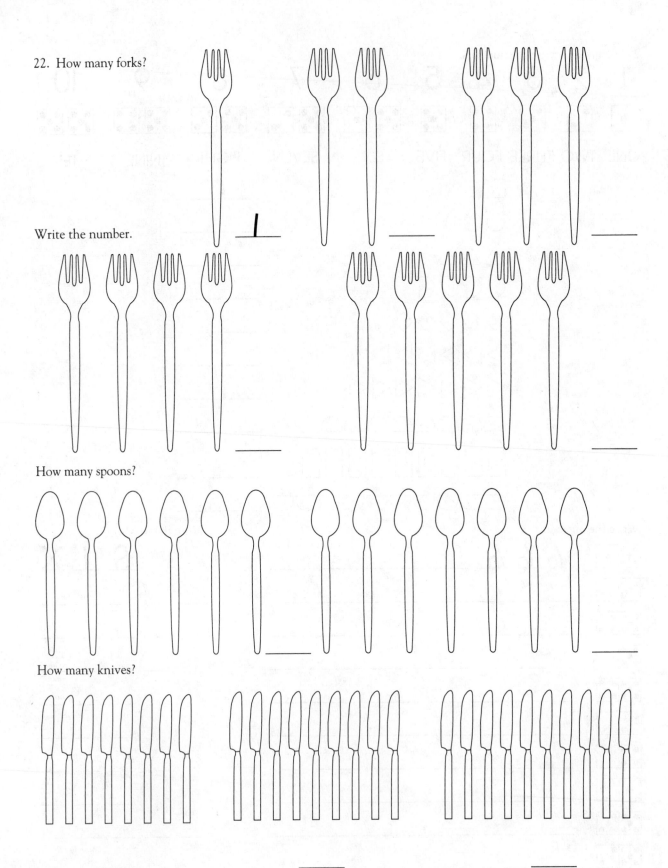

22. How many forks?

Write the number.

How many spoons?

How many knives?

NUMBERS 1–12 AND UPPER-CASE LETTERS

23. What time is it?
    Read and write the time.

6:00   7:00   8:00   9:00   10:00

1. __6:00__

2. __7:00__

3. __8:00__

4. __9:00__

5. __10:00__

6. _____

7. _____

8. _____

9. _____

10. _____

24. How much is this?

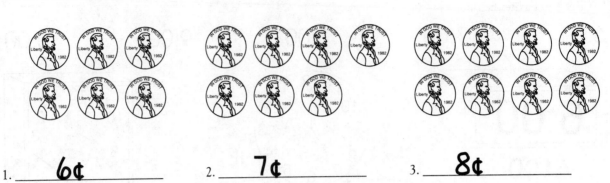

1. _____6¢_____   2. _____7¢_____   3. _____8¢_____

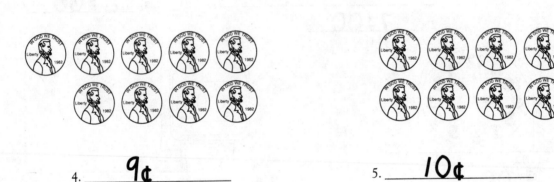

4. _____9¢_____   5. _____10¢_____

6. _____¢_____   7. _____

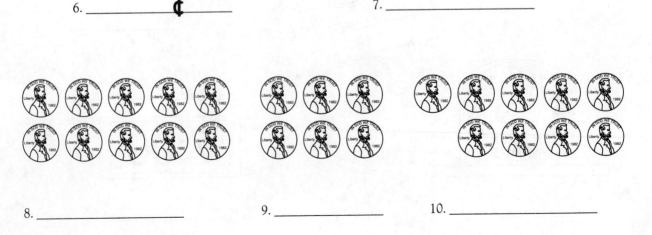

8. _____   9. _____   10. _____

25. Draw a line to the same number.

7	6	SEVEN	SIX
10	8	TEN	EIGHT
6	10	SIX	TEN
8	9	EIGHT	NINE
9	7	NINE	SEVEN

8	SIX		9
6	TEN		7
10	SEVEN		8
9	EIGHT		10
7	NINE		6

26. Look at the numbers and print the missing letters.

6 | | I | |

7 | S | | | |

8 | | | H | |

9 | N | | |

10 | | | N |

27. How much is this?

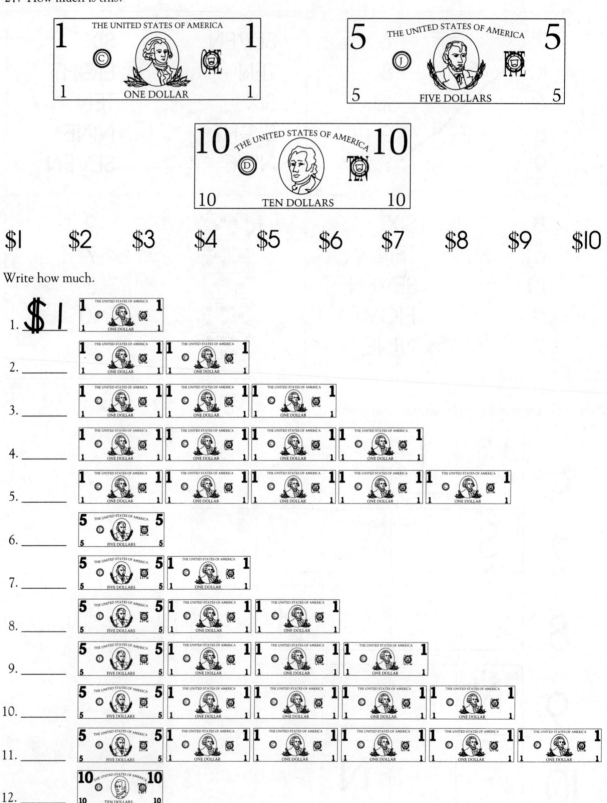

$1 $2 $3 $4 $5 $6 $7 $8 $9 $10

Write how much.

1. $1

2. _____

3. _____

4. _____

5. _____

6. _____

7. _____

8. _____

9. _____

10. _____

11. _____

12. _____

28. Copy the number.

11

Copy the letters.

E E

L L

Copy the word.

ELEVEN ELEVEN

Copy the number.

12 12 12

Copy the word.

TWELVE TWELVE

How much is this?

1. _____

2. _____

3. _____

4. _____

What time is it?

5. _____

6. _____

LITERACY IN LIFESKILLS

29. What time is it?

6:00   7:00   8:00   9:00   10:00   11:00   12:00

         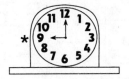

1. __6:00__   2. _____   3. _____   4. _____

   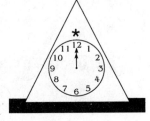   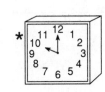

5. _____   6. _____   7. _____

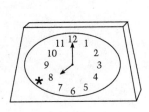   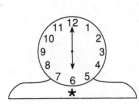

8. _____   9. _____   10. _____   11. _____

   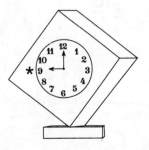   

12. _____   13. _____   14. _____

24

NUMBERS 1–12 AND UPPER-CASE LETTERS

30. Circle the same letter. Then say the letters.

T	E	(T)	L	G	(T)
R	O	I	R	U	R
V	V	E	V	X	G
N	T	N	S	R	N
G	V	G	W	P	E
W	H	W	F	U	X
I	T	F	I	N	L

31. Circle the letter your teacher says.

T	U	X
R	O	F
V	L	E
N	H	S
G	W	I

25

32. Circle the letter your teacher says. Then print the letter.

1	G	Ⓞ	W	O
2	G	O	W	
3	G	O	W	

1	I	T	V	
2	I	T	V	
3	I	T	V	

1	R	E	N	
2	R	E	N	
3	R	E	N	

1	U	F	L	
2	U	F	L	
3	U	F	L	

1	X	S	H	
2	X	S	H	
3	X	S	H	

Circle the number your teacher says. Then write the number.

1	1	3	5	
2	1	3	5	
3	1	3	5	

1	7	9	12	
2	7	9	12	
3	7	9	12	

1	10	4	6	
2	10	4	6	
3	10	4	6	

1	5	11	8	
2	5	11	8	
3	5	11	8	

33. Write either the letter or the number your teacher says.

1. N
2. 7
3. _____
4. _____
5. _____
6. _____

7. _____
8. _____
9. _____
10. _____
11. _____
12. _____

NUMBERS 1–12 AND UPPER-CASE LETTERS

34. Count and read the numbers.

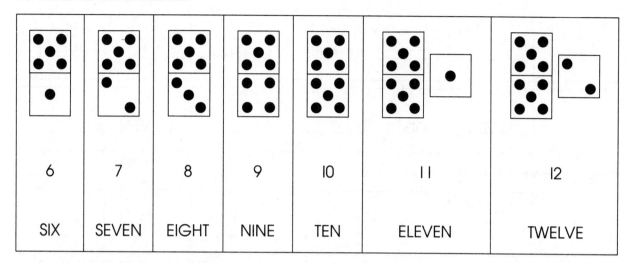

Write the numbers and print the words.

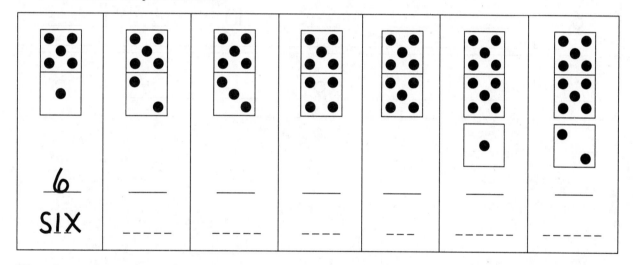

Write the numbers and print the words.

10	___	9	___	7	___
_ _ _	SIX	_ _ _ _	TWELVE	_ _ _ _ _	TEN
___	8	___	6	___	11
NINE	_ _ _ _ _	SEVEN	_ _ _	EIGHT	_ _ _ _ _ _

27

LITERACY IN LIFESKILLS

Print the words.

SIX	_ _ _ _ _	_ _ _ _ _	NINE	TEN	_ _ _ _ _ _	TWELVE

_ _ _	SEVEN	EIGHT	_ _ _ _	_ _ _	ELEVEN	_ _ _ _ _ _

Write the numbers.

6	7	8	___	___	11	___

6	___	___		10	___	___

___	___	___	9	___	___	12

¢ _____   :00 $ _____   :00

NUMBERS 1–12 AND UPPER-CASE LETTERS

35. Fill in the letters.

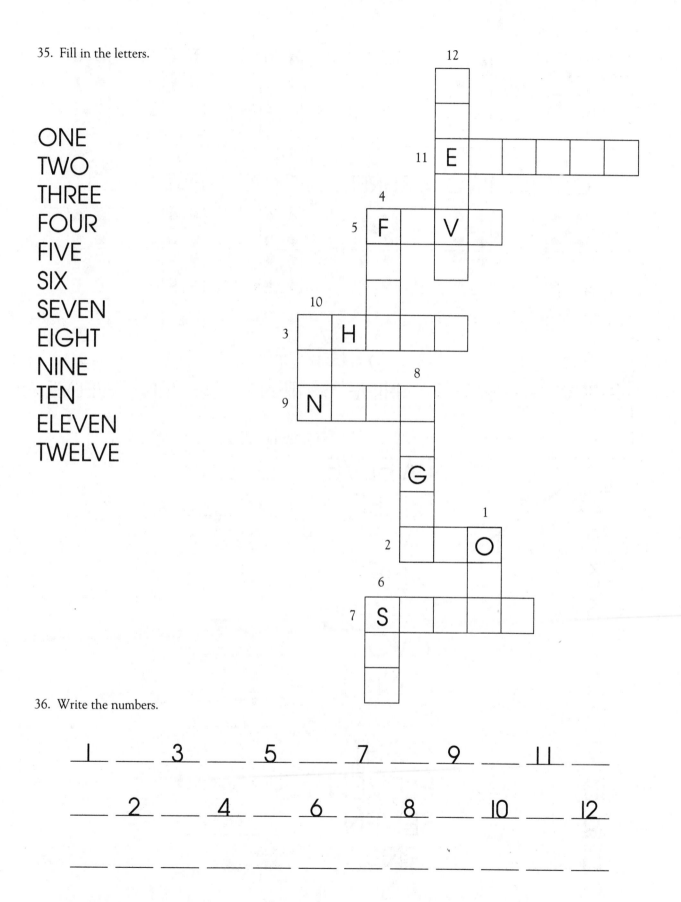

ONE
TWO
THREE
FOUR
FIVE
SIX
SEVEN
EIGHT
NINE
TEN
ELEVEN
TWELVE

36. Write the numbers.

1 ___ 3 ___ 5 ___ 7 ___ 9 ___ 11 ___

___ 2 ___ 4 ___ 6 ___ 8 ___ 10 ___ 12

___ ___ ___ ___ ___ ___ ___ ___ ___ ___ ___ ___

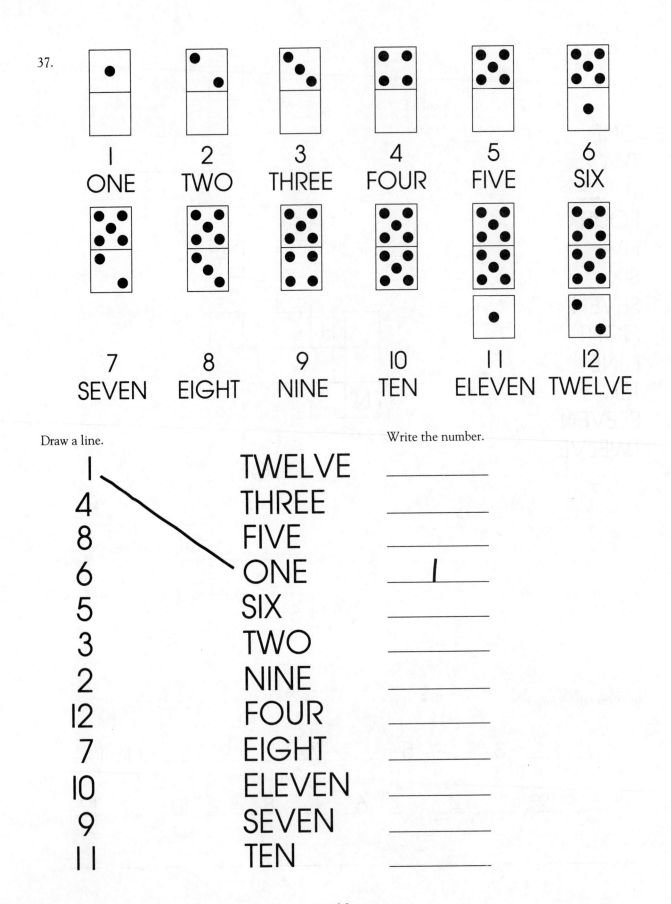

37.

1	2	3	4	5	6
ONE	TWO	THREE	FOUR	FIVE	SIX

7	8	9	10	11	12
SEVEN	EIGHT	NINE	TEN	ELEVEN	TWELVE

Draw a line.

	Write the number.
1 — TWELVE	_____
4 — THREE	_____
8 — FIVE	_____
6 — ONE	1
5 — SIX	_____
3 — TWO	_____
2 — NINE	_____
12 — FOUR	_____
7 — EIGHT	_____
10 — ELEVEN	_____
9 — SEVEN	_____
11 — TEN	_____

38. Write the numbers and print the words.

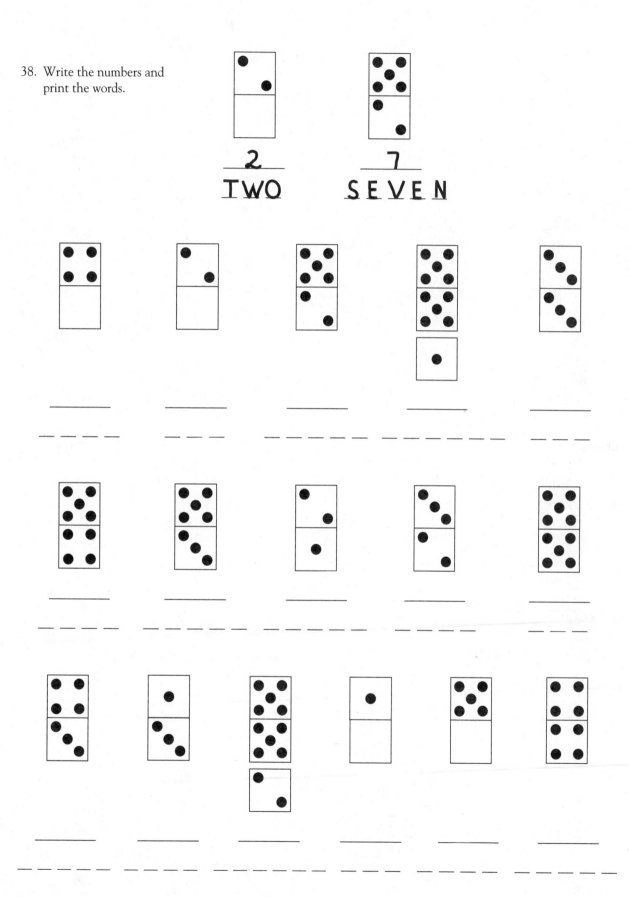

$\underline{2}$

TWO

$\underline{7}$

SEVEN

CHAPTER 2

THE
ALPHABET
AND YOUR
NAME

LITERACY IN LIFESKILLS

1. Copy the letters.

G

O

D

M

R

N

I

Copy the words.

GOOD MORNING

Copy the letters.

A

F

T

E

Copy the words.

GOOD AFTERNOON

34

Copy the letter.

V

Copy the words.

GOOD EVENING

Copy the letters.

B

Y

Copy the words.

GOOD—BYE

Copy the letter.

H

Copy the words.

GOOD NIGHT

GOOD MORNING
GOOD AFTERNOON
GOOD EVENING
GOOD—BYE
GOOD NIGHT

A B C D E F G H I J K L M N O P Q R S T U V W X Y Z

2. Copy the letters.

A A _____

B B _____

C C _____

D D _____

E E _____

F F _____

G G _____

H H _____

I I _____ I I _____

J J _____

K K _____

L L _____

M M _____

N N _____

O O _____

P P --

Q Q --

R R --

S S --

T T --

U U --

V V --

W W --

X X --

Y Y --

Z Z --

3. Print the letters.

A A   B _   C _   D _   E _   F _   G _

H _   I _   J _   K _   L _   M _   N _

O _   P _   Q _   R _   S _   T _   U _

V _   W _   X _   Y _   Z _

4. Copy the letters.

N

A

M

E

Copy your name from your name card. Copy other names.

NAME

5. How are you?
   Listen, repeat, and answer.

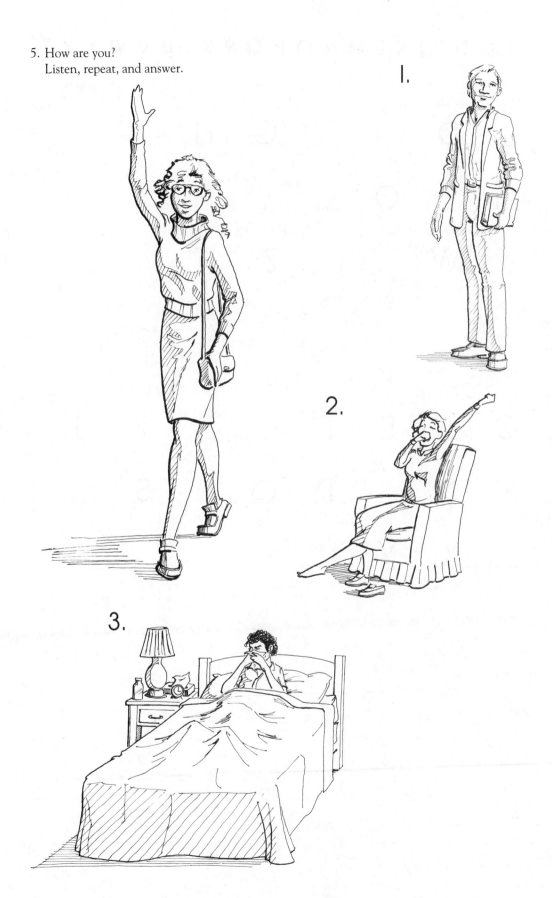

A B C D E F G H I J K L M N O P Q R S T U V W X Y Z

6. Print the letters.

A B _ D _ _ G H _ _

K L M _ O _ _ R S

T _ _ W _ _ Z

_ _ C _ E F _ _ I J

_ _ _ N _ P Q _ S _

U V _ X Y _

A _ _ _ _ _ _ _ _

_ _ _ _ _ _ _ _

_ _ _ _ _ _ _ _

THE ALPHABET AND YOUR NAME

7. Circle the letters your teacher says. Then print the letters.

1. A (B) C D   **B**
2. A B C D
3. A B C D
4. A B C D
5. A B C D

1. E F G H
2. E F G H
3. E F G H
4. E F G H

1. I J K L
2. I J K L
3. I J K L
4. I J K L
5. I J K L

1. M N O P
2. M N O P
3. M N O P
4. M N O P

1. Q R S T
2. Q R S T
3. Q R S T
4. Q R S T

1. U V W
2. U V W
3. U V W

1. X Y Z
2. X Y Z
3. X Y Z

STOP 8. Print the groups of letters your teacher says.

1. POB
2. _____
3. _____
4. _____
5. _____
6. _____

9. Listen and repeat the letters.

C C	C G	G G	G C
B B	B D	D D	D B
D D	D V	V V	V D
S F	F F	S S	F S
A H	H H	A A	H A
P T	T T	P P	T P
C Z	C C	Z Z	Z C
G J	J J	G G	J G
M N	M M	N N	N M
O R	O O	R R	R O
K Q	K K	Q Q	Q K
X S	X X	S S	S X
I Y	I I	Y Y	Y I
V B	V V	B B	B V
T D	D D	T T	D T

STOP 10. Print the letters your teacher says.

1. _____   6. _____

2. _____   7. _____

3. _____   8. _____

4. _____   9. _____

5. _____   10. _____

11. Circle the same letter. Then print the letter.

W	A	C	M	(W)	T	**W**
A	H	B	V	R	A	
I	I	L	H	F	T	
Y	X	K	R	V	Y	
U	U	V	W	J	B	
R	D	P	B	R	K	
F	E	P	R	T	F	
E	P	L	C	E	G	

H	W	H	N	M	B	
T	L	A	T	E	F	
S	B	R	G	S	C	
O	S	C	O	Q	G	
R	D	P	B	R	K	
M	Z	W	N	K	M	
N	N	W	M	V	Z	
L	E	I	K	T	L	

12. Sing the song.

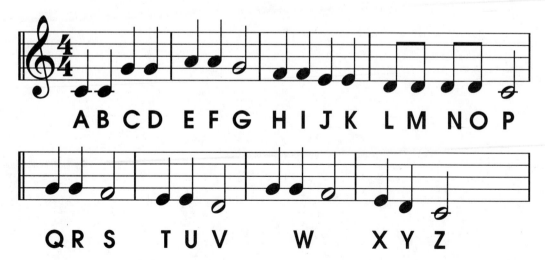

MY NAME IS SUE LEE.

GOOD EVENING.

HI. I AM SALLY.

WHAT IS YOUR FIRST NAME?

HELLO.

GOOD AFTERNOON

CHAPTER 3

▲▲▲▲▲▲▲▲

INTRODUCTIONS

HI.

GOOD MORNING.

HOW DO YOU DO?

GOOD-BYE

FINE, THANK YOU.

HOW ARE YOU?

MY NAME IS DAN.

NICE TO MEET YOU.

HIS LAST NAME IS HALL.

HER FIRST NAME IS SUE.

WHAT IS YOUR LAST NAME?

1. Say the letters and copy the words.

MY   MY --

FIRST   FIRST ---

NAME   NAME --

IS   IS --

Print the letters and read the words. Then print your first name.

1. | MY | FIRST | NAME | IS | ============================= | .

2. | M_ | F_R_T | N_M_ | I_ | ----------------------------- | .

3. | _Y | _I_ST | _A_E_S | ----------------------------- | _

4. | M_ | F____ | N____ | I_ | ----------------------------- | _

5. | MY | _____ | NAME | __ | ----------------------------- | _

6. | __ | FIRST | ____ | IS | ----------------------------- | .

7. | __ | ____ | ____ | __ | ----------------------------- | _

2. Say the letters and copy the words.

WHAT   WHAT

IS   IS

YOUR   YOUR

FIRST   FIRST

NAME   NAME

?   ?

Print the letters and read the words. Then print your first name.

1. WHAT IS YOUR FIRST NAME ?

2. W_A_ I_ Y_U_ F_R_T N_M_ _

3. _H_T __ _O_R _I_S_ _A_E ?

4. WHAT __ YOUR _____ NAME _

5. _____ IS _____ FIRST _____ _

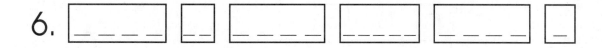

6. _____ __ _____ _____ _____ _

3. Print the words. Then print your first name.

A. **FIRST NAME**

B. F_RST NAME

C. _IRST NAME

D. FI_ST NAME

E. FIR_T NAME

F. FIRS_ NAME

G. _ _ _ _ _ _ _ _ _

H. MY **FIRST** NAME IS _____.

Print the words. Then print your last name.

I. **LAST NAME**

J. L_ST NAME

K. _AST NAME

L. LA_ _ NAME

M. LAS_ NAME

N. _ _ _ _ _ _ _ _

O. MY **LAST** NAME IS _____.

4. Print the letters.

FIRST
LAST
NAME

		A	

| F | | | |

5. Read.

A: WHAT IS YOUR **FIRST** NAME?

B: MY **FIRST** NAME IS SUE.

A: WHAT IS YOUR **LAST** NAME?

B: MY **LAST** NAME IS LEE.

6. Read and print *your* own first and last name.

1. WHAT IS YOUR **FIRST** NAME?

2. MY **FIRST** NAME IS_____.

3. WHAT IS YOUR **LAST** NAME?

4. MY **LAST** NAME IS_____.

7. Print your name.

FIRST NAME_____

LAST NAME_____

8. Read and copy the words. Then complete the sentences with your name.

A. WHAT IS YOUR **FIRST** NAME ?

B. WHAT IS ____ ____ ____ __

C. MY **FIRST** NAME IS _____ .

D. __ __ ____ ____ ____ __ __ _____ __

E. WHAT IS YOUR **LAST** NAME ?

F. ____ __ ____ __ ____ ____ ____

G. MY **LAST** NAME IS _____ .

H. __ __ ____ ____ ____ ____ __

I. W___ IS YOUR **FIRST** NAME ?

J. MY **FIRST** NAME IS _____ .

K. _____ IS YOUR **LAST** NAME ?

L. __ **LAST** NAME IS _____ .

M. WHAT IS Y____ **FIRST** NAME ?

N. MY **FIRST** NAME __ _____ .

O. WHAT IS _____ **LAST** NAME ?

P. MY **LAST** NAME __ _____ .

Q. MY FIRST N____ IS _____ .

R. MY **LAST** _____ IS _____ .

9. Circle the words your teacher says.

WHAT	?	LAST
FIRST	IS	MY
YOUR	.	NAME

10. Circle the letters your teacher says.

W	H	A	T	J
I	S	Y	O	Q
U	R	N	M	K
E	F	.	?	X
L	D	P	C	G

11. Print your name.

FIRST NAME _____

LAST NAME _____

12. Listen and repeat.

A: HI. MY NAME IS SALLY.
B: NICE TO MEET YOU.
A: NICE TO MEET YOU.

A

B

13. Read.

A: HI. WHAT IS YOUR FIRST NAME?

B: MY FIRST NAME IS SUE.

A: SPELL YOUR FIRST NAME.

B: S U E

A: SPELL YOUR LAST NAME.

B: L E E

A   B

Copy.

1. HI . WHAT IS YOUR FIRST NAME ?
2. __ _ ____ __ ___ ____ ____ _
3. MY NAME IS SUE .
4. __ ____ __ ___ _
5. SPELL YOUR FIRST NAME .
6. _____ ____ ____ ____ _
7. S U E
8. _ _ _
9. SPELL YOUR LAST NAME .
10. _____ ____ ____ ____ _
11. L E E
12. _ _ _

14. Read the words. Then print your name.

1. WHAT IS YOUR FIRST NAME?

2. MY FIRST NAME IS _____.

3. **SPELL** YOUR FIRST NAME.

4.

FIRST NAME

5. WHAT IS YOUR LAST NAME?

6. MY LAST NAME IS _____.

7. **SPELL** YOUR LAST NAME.

8.

LAST NAME

9.

FIRST   LAST

15. Read.

A: HOW DO YOU DO?

B: HOW DO YOU DO?

A: MY NAME IS DAN.

B: MY NAME IS SUE.

A: NICE TO MEET YOU.

B: NICE TO MEET YOU.

A   B

16. Read, copy, and fill in the words.

1. HOW DO YOU DO ?

2. H OW __ __ ___ __ __ _

3. NICE TO MEET YOU .

4. ____ __ ____ ___ _

5. WHAT __ YOUR NAME ?

6. MY NAME IS _____.

7. SPELL YOUR FIRST _ _ _ _ .

8.
FIRST NAME

9. HOW __ __ YOU DO ?

10. NICE __ __ ____ ___ .

17. Read.

A: MY NAME IS SUE LEE.
MY FIRST NAME IS SUE.

B: **HER** FIRST NAME IS SUE.

Copy.

1. WHAT IS **HER** FIRST NAME ?

2. _ _ _ _   _ _   _ _ _   _ _ _ _   _ _ _ _   _

3. **HER** FIRST NAME IS SUE .

4. _ _ _   _ _ _ _ _   _ _ _ _   _ _   _ _ _   _

Read.

A: MY NAME IS SUE LEE.
MY LAST NAME IS LEE.

B: **HER** LAST NAME IS LEE.

Copy.

5. WHAT IS **HER** LAST NAME ?

6. _ _ _ _   _ _   _ _ _   _ _ _ _   _ _ _ _   _

7. **HER** LAST NAME IS LEE .

8. _ _ _   _ _ _ _   _ _ _ _   _ _   _ _ _   _

INTRODUCTIONS

18. Fill in the missing words.

1. **HER** FIRST NAME IS SUE.
2. _ _ _ FIRST NAME IS SUE.
3. **HER** _ _ _ _ _ NAME IS **SUE**.
4. **HER** _ _ _ _ NAME IS **LEE**.
5. **HER** FIRST _ _ _ _ IS SUE.
6. **HER** LAST _ _ _ _ IS LEE.
7. **HER** FIRST NAME IS _ _ _ .
8. **HER** LAST NAME IS _ _ _ .
9. _ _ _ FIRST NAME IS _ _ _ .
10. _ _ _ LAST NAME IS _ _ _ .
11. _ _ _ NAME IS **S** _ _ **L** _ _ .

SUE LEE

19. Print your name.

FIRST NAME

LAST NAME

NAME

FIRST   LAST

57

20. Read.

A: MY NAME IS DAN HALL.
   MY FIRST NAME IS DAN.

B: **HIS** FIRST NAME IS DAN.

Copy.

1. WHAT IS **HIS** FIRST NAME ?

2. _ _ _ _   _ _   _ _ _   _ _ _ _   _ _ _ _   _

3. **HIS** FIRST NAME IS DAN .

4. _ _ _   _ _ _ _ _   _ _ _ _   _ _   _ _ _   _

Read.

A: MY NAME IS DAN HALL.
   MY LAST NAME IS HALL.

B: **HIS** LAST NAME IS HALL.

Copy.

5. WHAT IS **HIS** LAST NAME ?

6. _ _ _ _   _ _   _ _ _   _ _ _ _   _ _ _ _   _

7. **HIS** LAST NAME IS HALL .

8. _ _ _   _ _ _ _   _ _ _ _   _ _   _ _ _ _   _

21. Fill in the missing words.

1. **HIS** FIRST NAME IS DAN.
2. _ _ _ FIRST NAME IS DAN.
3. **HIS** _ _ _ _ _ NAME IS **DAN**.
4. **HIS** _ _ _ _ NAME IS **HALL**.
5. **HIS** FIRST _ _ _ _ IS DAN.
6. **HIS** LAST _ _ _ _ IS HALL.
7. **HIS** FIRST NAME IS _ _ _ .
8. **HIS** LAST NAME IS _ _ _ _ .
9. _ _ _ FIRST NAME IS _ _ _ .
10. _ _ _ LAST NAME IS _ _ _ _ .
11. _ _ _ NAME _ _ **D** _ _ **H** _ _ _ .

DAN HALL

22. Print your name.

LAST NAME																				

FIRST NAME																				

NAME																						

LAST   FIRST

23. Read.

GOOD MORNING   GOOD AFTERNOON   GOOD EVENING

1   2   3

24. Read.

A: GOOD MORNING.
B: GOOD MORNING.

A: HOW ARE YOU?
B: FINE, THANK YOU, AND YOU?

A: FINE, THANK YOU.

A   B

25. Fill in the missing words.

1. G _ _ _ MORNING.
2. GOOD M_ _ _ _ _ _.
3. HOW A_ _ Y_ _?
4. FINE, T _ _ _ _ _ Y _ _,
   AND Y_ _?
5. F_ _ _, TH_ _ _ Y_ _.

6. G_ _ _ AFTERNOON.
7. G_ _ _ A_ _ _ _ _ _ _ _.
8. H_ _ ARE _ _U?
9. _ _ _ _, THANK _ _ _,
   _ _ _ YOU?
10. F_ _ _, T_ _ _ _ Y_ _.

1. G_ _ _ EVENING.
2. GOOD E_ _ _ _ _ _.
3. _ _ _ A _ _ YOU?
4. _ _ _ _, TH_ _ _ YOU,
   A_ _ Y_ _?
5. F_ _ _, _ _ _ _ _ YOU.

6.   GOOD-BYE.
   _ _ _ _ - _ _ _.

7. GOOD NIGHT.
   G_ _ _ N_ _ _ _.

60

26. Listen and repeat.

A: GOOD MORNING.
B: GOOD MORNING.

A: GET UP.
B: WHAT TIME IS IT?

A: 7:00
B: OK.

27. Listen and repeat.

A: GOOD NIGHT.
B: GOOD NIGHT.

A: GO TO SLEEP.
B: WHAT TIME IS IT?

A: 10:00
B: OK. GOOD NIGHT.

28. Review Exercises. Print the letters.

A   B   _   D   _   F   _   _   I   _
K   _   M   _   _   P   _   _   _
T   _   V   _   _   Y

Print the words.

1. HOW _____ YOU DO?
2. NICE _____ _____ YOU.

3. GOOD _____.
4. HOW _____ YOU?
5. FINE, _____ YOU.

Fill in the missing words.

6. _____ IS YOUR FIRST NAME?

7. _____ FIRST NAME IS_____.

8. WHAT IS _____ LAST NAME?

9. MY LAST _____ IS _____.

Write the numbers.

1 _ _ _ _ 6 _ _ _ _ _ _

Please print.

NAME_____
           FIRST   LAST

NAME_____, _____
           LAST   FIRST

WHAT IS YOUR SOCIAL SECURITY NUMBER?

268-47-3596

SOCIAL SECURITY

560-56-5656

SUE LEE
NAME

WHAT LANGUAGE DO YOU SPEAK?

HIS SOCIAL SECURITY NUMBER IS 560-56-1234.

SOCIAL SECURITY

532-46-1379

DAVE HAPPY
NAME

CHAPTER 4

▲▲▲▲▲▲▲▲

PERSONAL INFORMATION

FIRST NAME_____
LAST NAME_____
TELEPHONE NUMBER
_____

892-97-9345

622-5830

570-3466

I SPEAK FRENCH.

I DON'T HAVE A
TELEPHONE.

I DON'T HAVE A
SOCIAL SECURITY
NUMBER.

958-7654

I SPEAK A LITTLE ENGLISH.

WHAT IS YOUR TELEPHONE NUMBER?

I AM FROM CHINA.

I SPEAK SPANISH.

WHAT COUNTRY ARE YOU FROM?

HER TELEPHONE NUMBER IS 431-2200.

1. Write your telephone number.

WHAT IS YOUR TELEPHONE NUMBER ?

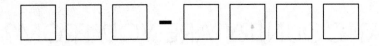

2. Write your telephone number.

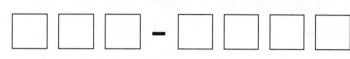

TELEPHONE NUMBER

☐ ☐ ☐ – ☐ ☐ ☐ ☐

Circle the numbers in your telephone number.

1 2 3 4 5 6 7 8 9 0

3. Read.

A B

A: WHAT IS YOUR **TELEPHONE NUMBER?**
B: MY **TELEPHONE NUMBER** IS 781-9540.
   WHAT IS YOUR **PHONE NUMBER?**
A: I DON'T HAVE A **PHONE.**

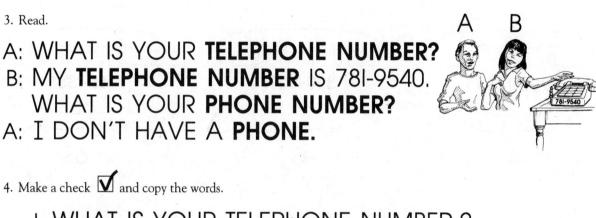

4. Make a check and copy the words.

    1. WHAT IS YOUR TELEPHONE NUMBER ?
    2. **WHAT** __ ____ _____ _____ _
☐ 3. MY TELEPHONE NUMBER IS ☐☐☐-☐☐☐☐.
    4. __ _____ _____ __ ☐☐☐-☐☐☐☐.
☐ 5. I DON'T HAVE A PHONE .
    6. _ ____'_ ____ _ _____ _

5. Read these telephone numbers.

STOP

6. Write the phone numbers your teacher says.

1. 570-3466
2. 431-2200
3. 958-7654
4. 329-0105
5. 622-5830
6. 287-0733

1. 828-1_45
2. 6_2-8990
3. 35_-6206
4. 747-_551
5. 993-25__
6. ____-____

7. Read.

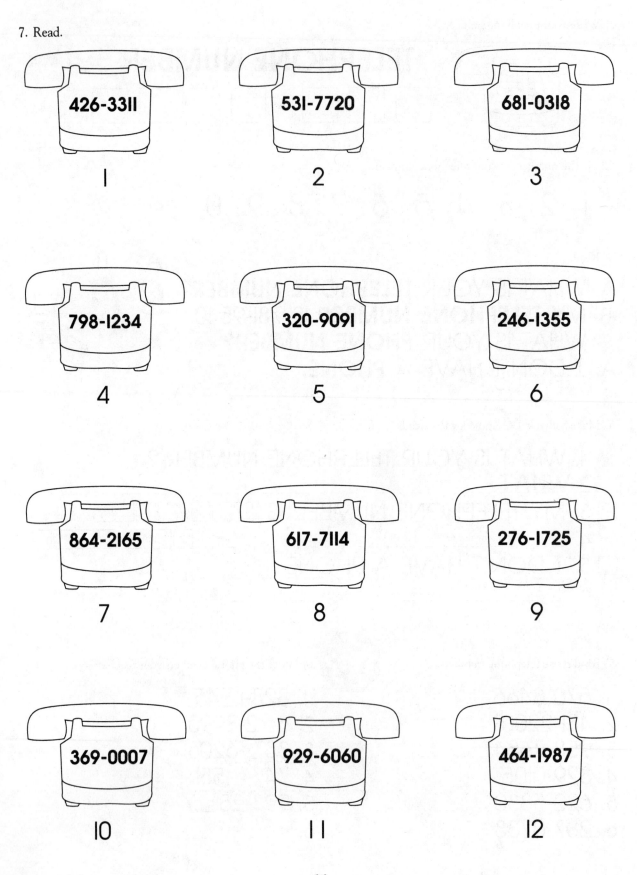

1. 426-3311

2. 531-7720

3. 681-0318

4. 798-1234

5. 320-9091

6. 246-1355

7. 864-2165

8. 617-7114

9. 276-1725

10. 369-0007

11. 929-6060

12. 464-1987

8. Read and copy the sentences.

1. **HIS** TELEPHONE NUMBER IS 553-2406.

2. ___ _____ _____ __ □□□-□□□□.

3. **HER** TELEPHONE NUMBER IS 781-9540.

4. ___ _____ _____ __ □□□-□□□□.

Read and complete the answers to the questions.

5. WHAT IS **HIS** TELEPHONE NUMBER?

6. ___ TELEPHONE NUMBER IS 553-2406.

7. WHAT IS **HER** TELEPHONE NUMBER?

8. ___ TELEPHONE NUMBER IS 781-9540.

9. **HER** PHONE NUMBER IS 848-8467.

10. **HIS** PHONE NUMBER IS □□□-□□□□.

Look at the pictures and fill in the sentences.

11. ___ PHONE NUMBER IS □□□-□□□□.

12. ___ PHONE NUMBER IS □□□-□□□□.

9. Fill out this form.

FIRST NAME _____
LAST NAME _____
TELEPHONE NUMBER _____

10. Print the words and write the numbers.

ONE	F IVE	SIX	_ _ _ _	TWELVE
1	5	_	4	_
_ _ _	ELEVEN	_ _ _ _ _	EIGHT	_ _ _
6	_	3	_	10
_ _ _ _ _	TEN	▨	TWO	_ _ _ _
8	_		_	9
THREE	_ _ _	FOUR	_ _ _	SEVEN
_	2	_	1	_
_ _ _ _ _	NINE	_ _ _ _ _	FIVE	_ _ _ _ _
12	_	7	_	11

1 _ 3 _ _ 6 7 _ 9 _ 11 _
_ 2 _ 4 5 _ _ 8 _ 10 _ 12

_ _ _ _ _ _ _ _ _ _ _ _

11. Read these social security numbers.

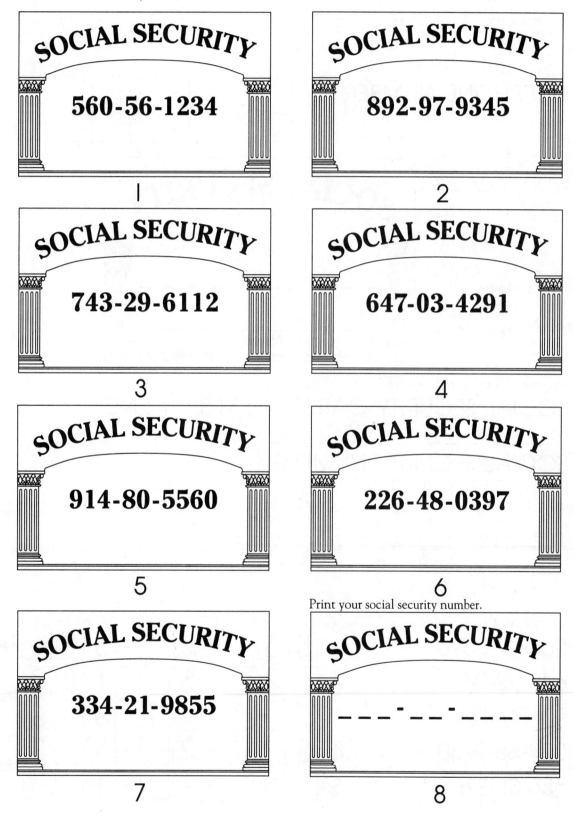

SOCIAL SECURITY

560-56-1234

1

SOCIAL SECURITY

892-97-9345

2

SOCIAL SECURITY

743-29-6112

3

SOCIAL SECURITY

647-03-4291

4

SOCIAL SECURITY

914-80-5560

5

SOCIAL SECURITY

226-48-0397

6

SOCIAL SECURITY

334-21-9855

7

Print your social security number.

SOCIAL SECURITY

_ _ _ - _ _ - _ _ _ _

8

12. Make a check ☑. Copy the words. Write your number.

1. [telephone] ☐ YES   ☐ NO

2. TELEPHONE NUMBER ☐☐☐ - ☐☐☐☐

3. _ _ _ _ _ _ _ _ _ _ _ _ _ _ _ ☐☐☐ - ☐☐☐☐

SOCIAL SECURITY

13. Print your number. 1.

_ _ _ - _ _ - _ _ _ _

   Print your name. 2.

_____
NAME

Make a check ☑ and copy the words.

3. SOCIAL SECURITY CARD   ☐ YES   ☐ NO

4. _ _ _ _ _ _ _ _ _ _ _ _ _ _ _ _ _ _

5. SOCIAL SECURITY NUMBER

☐☐☐ - ☐☐ - ☐☐☐☐

6. _ _ _ _ _ _ _ _ _ _ _ _ _ _ _ _ _ _

☐☐☐ - ☐☐ - ☐☐☐☐

STOP

14. Read the social security numbers.

1. 268-47-3596

2. 648-92-0477

3. 931-50-4246

4. 024-55-9730

5. 556-31-1221

15. Write the social security numbers your teacher says.

1. 5 5 ☐ - 2 ☐ - 3 3 4 4

2. 6 2 ☐ - 5 ☐ - 1 8 0 ☐

3. 3 ☐ 9 - ☐ 7 - 8 ☐ 6

4. 8 ☐ ☐ - 2 ☐ - ☐ ☐ 3

5. ☐ ☐ ☐ - 1 ☐ - 4 ☐ ☐

70

16. Read.

A: WHAT IS YOUR SOCIAL SECURITY NUMBER?
B: 560-56-5656
    WHAT IS YOUR SOCIAL SECURITY NUMBER?
A: I DON'T HAVE A SOCIAL SECURITY NUMBER.

17. Make a check ✓ and copy the words.

    1. WHAT IS YOUR **SOCIAL SECURITY** NUMBER ?
    2. W___ __ ____ _____ _____ ____ _

☐ 3. MY SOCIAL SECURITY NUMBER IS

    ☐☐☐ - ☐☐ - ☐☐☐☐.

    4. __ _____ _____ _____ __

    ☐☐☐ - ☐☐ - ☐☐☐☐.

☐ 5. I DON'T HAVE A SOCIAL SECURITY NUMBER.
    6. _ ___'_ ____ _ _____ _____ _____.
☐ 7. I DON'T KNOW.
    8. _ ___'_ ____ _

18. Look at the pictures and write the social security numbers.

    1. **HIS** SOCIAL SECURITY NUMBER IS ☐☐☐ - ☐☐ - ☐☐☐☐.

    2. **HER** SOCIAL SECURITY NUMBER IS ☐☐☐ - ☐☐ - ☐☐☐☐.

    3. **MY** SOCIAL SECURITY NUMBER IS ☐☐☐ - ☐☐ - ☐☐☐☐.

71

19. Write the words.

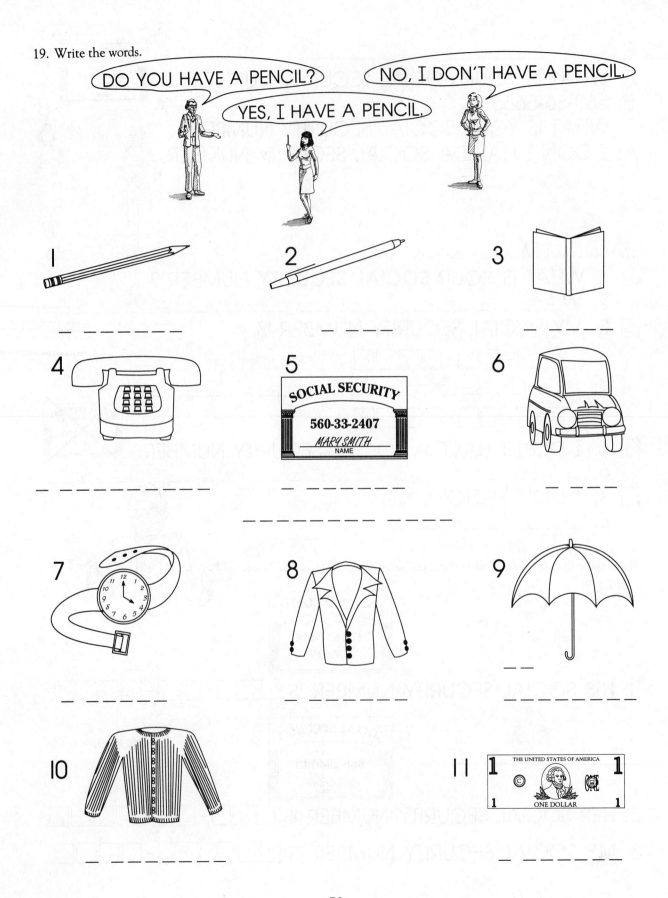

20. Read.

1. A: WHAT LANGUAGE DO YOU SPEAK?
   B: I SPEAK CHINESE.

2. A: WHAT LANGUAGE DO YOU SPEAK?
   C: I SPEAK SPANISH.

3. A: WHAT LANGUAGE DO YOU SPEAK?
   D: I SPEAK ENGLISH.

4. A: DO YOU SPEAK ENGLISH?
   E: YES. I SPEAK A LITTLE ENGLISH.

A B

A C

A D

A E

21. Copy the words. Then make a check ✔.

1. WHAT LANGUAGE DO YOU SPEAK ?

2. ____ _____ __ ___ _____ _

3. I SPEAK
   ☐ CHINESE   ☐ SPANISH   ☐ VIETNAMESE
   ☐ JAPANESE   ☐ FRENCH   ☐ ARABIC
   ☐ KOREAN   ☐ GERMAN   ☐ ENGLISH
   ☐ _____

4. I SPEAK _____ .

5. _ _____ _____ .

6. DO YOU SPEAK ENGLISH ?

7. __ ___ _____ _____ _

8. ☐ YES   ☐ NO   ☐ YES, A LITTLE.
   ___   __   ___, _ _____ .

22. Fill out the form.

FIRST NAME _____
LAST NAME _____
TELEPHONE NUMBER _____
SOCIAL SECURITY NUMBER _____
LANGUAGE _____

23. Read.

1. A: WHAT COUNTRY ARE YOU FROM?
    B: I AM FROM CHINA.

2. A: WHAT COUNTRY ARE YOU FROM?
    C: I AM FROM MEXICO.

3. A: WHAT COUNTRY ARE YOU FROM?
    D: I AM FROM THE UNITED STATES.
    A: THE U.S.?
    D: YES, THE UNITED STATES OF AMERICA.

24. Copy the words and make a check ☑ .

1. WHAT COUNTRY ARE YOU FROM ?

2. _

3. I AM FROM
   - ☐ CHINA   ☐ MEXICO   ☐ VIETNAM
   - ☐ JAPAN   ☐ EL SALVADOR   ☐ BURMA
   - ☐ KOREA   ☐ THE PHILIPPINES   ☐ FRANCE
   - ☐ LAOS   ☐ ETHIOPIA   ☐ THE U.S.
   - ☐ _____

4. I AM FROM _____ .

5. _ _ _ _ _ _ _ _ _____ .

25. Fill out the form.

SOCIAL SECURITY NUMBER ☐☐☐ - ☐☐ - ☐☐☐☐

TELEPHONE NUMBER ☐☐☐ - ☐☐☐☐

LANGUAGE ☐☐☐☐☐☐☐☐☐☐☐☐☐☐☐☐☐

LAST NAME ☐☐☐☐☐☐☐☐☐☐☐☐☐☐☐☐☐

FIRST NAME ☐☐☐☐☐☐☐☐☐☐☐☐☐☐☐☐☐

COUNTRY ☐☐☐☐☐☐☐☐☐☐☐☐☐☐☐☐☐☐

26. Read.

A: MY NAME IS <u>SUE</u> **ELLEN** <u>LEE</u>.
              FIRST   MIDDLE   LAST

B: WHAT IS YOUR **MIDDLE** NAME?

A: MY **MIDDLE** NAME IS ELLEN.
    WHAT IS YOUR **MIDDLE** NAME?

B: I DON'T HAVE A **MIDDLE** NAME.

27. Read and copy the sentences. Then make a check ☑ .

   1. WHAT IS YOUR **MIDDLE** NAME ?

   2. ____ __ ____ _____ ____ _

☐ 3. MY **MIDDLE** NAME IS _____.

   4. __ _____ ____ __ _____ _

☐ 5. I DON'T HAVE A **MIDDLE** NAME.

   6. _ ____'_ ____ _ _____ ____ _

28. Print your name. If you don't have a middle name, draw a long line.

FIRST NAME _____

MIDDLE NAME _____

LAST NAME _____

29. Print the letters.

NAME
FIRST
MIDDLE
LAST

30. Print your name. If you don't have a middle name, draw a long line.

NAME _____
      FIRST   MIDDLE   LAST

NAME _____
      LAST   FIRST   MIDDLE

31. Answer the questions.

1. WHAT IS YOUR FIRST NAME?
2. MY FIRST NAME IS _____.

3. WHAT LANGUAGE DO YOU SPEAK?
4. I SPEAK _____.

5. WHAT IS YOUR TELEPHONE NUMBER?
6. ☐☐☐ - ☐☐☐☐

7. WHAT COUNTRY ARE YOU FROM?
8. I AM FROM _____.

9. DO YOU SPEAK ENGLISH?
10. ☐ NO. I DON'T SPEAK _____.
    ☐ YES. I SPEAK A LITTLE _____.

11. HOW ARE YOU?
12. FINE, _____ _____.

13. GOOD-BYE.
14. ____ - ___.

32. Fill out the forms.

I.

NAME _____
        FIRST   MIDDLE   LAST
TELEPHONE NUMBER ___-____
SOCIAL SECURITY NUMBER ___-__-____
COUNTRY _____
LANGUAGE _____

2.

☐☐☐☐☐☐☐☐☐☐☐☐☐☐☐☐☐☐☐☐☐☐☐☐☐☐
        LAST NAME   FIRST NAME
SOC. SEC. NUMBER ☐☐☐-☐☐-☐☐☐☐
PHONE ☐☐☐-☐☐☐☐
LANGUAGE ☐☐☐☐☐☐☐☐☐☐☐☐☐☐☐☐☐
COUNTRY ☐☐☐☐☐☐☐☐☐☐☐☐☐☐☐☐☐

33. Print the colors on the lines.

COLORS

1. BLACK
2. PINK
3. GRAY
4. BROWN
5. ORANGE
6. PURPLE
7. WHITE
8. YELLOW
9. GREEN
10. BLUE
11. RED

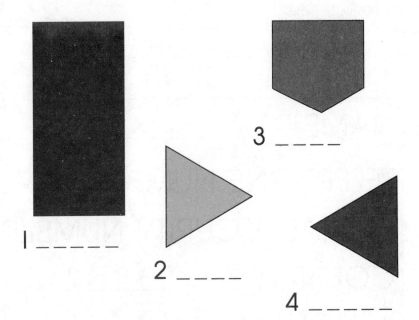

1 _ _ _ _ _

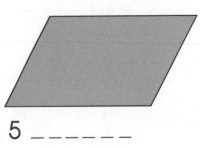

2 _ _ _ _

3 _ _ _ _

4 _ _ _ _ _

5 _ _ _ _ _ _

6 _ _ _ _ _ _

7 _ _ _ _ _

8 _ _ _ _ _ _

9 _ _ _ _ _

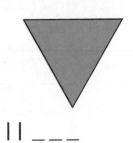

10 _ _ _ _

11 _ _ _

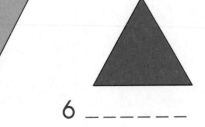

34. Write the color.

WHAT COLOR IS THE PENCIL?

YELLOW

1 _ _ _ _ _ _

2 _ _ _ _ _

3 _ _ _ _ _ _

4 _ _ _ _ _

SOCIAL SECURITY
560-56-5656
SUE ELLEN LEE
SUE ELLEN LEE

5 _ _ _ _

6 _ _ _ _

7 _ _ _ _ _

8 _ _ _ _ _

9 _ _ _ _ _ _

10 _ _ _ _ _

APPLE

_ _ _ _ _

11 _ _ _

79

35. Listen and repeat.

WHAT COLOR IS THE AMERICAN FLAG?

_ _ _

_ _ _ _ _

AND _ _ _ _ _

36. Read and copy the words.

1. STOP
2. WALK
3. WALK
4. DON'T WALK
5. STOP
6. BE CAREFUL
7. GO

1. _ _ _ _

2. _ _ _ _

WALK

DON'T
WALK

3. _ _ _ _ _   4. _ _ _ _ _ _ _ _ _

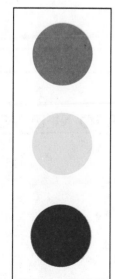

5. _ _ _ _ _

6. _ _ _ _ _ _ _ _ _ _

7. _ _

37. Read and copy the words.

T

1. 2 TWO _____

2. TIME

WHAT **TIME** IS IT?

3. 10 TEN _____

4. TELEPHONE

WHAT IS YOUR **TELEPHONE** NUMBER?

MY **TELEPHONE** NUMBER IS 264-0722.

5. TO _____

HOW DO YOU DO?

NICE **TO** MEET YOU.

T	TWO
	TIME
	TEN
	TELEPHONE
	TO

38. Read and copy the words.

F

1. 4 FOUR _____
2. 5 FIVE _____
3. FORK _____

I HAVE A SPOON AND A KNIFE.

I HAVE A **FORK**.

4. FIRST _____

WHAT IS YOUR **FIRST** NAME?

MY **FIRST** NAME IS SUE.

5. FINE _____

HOW ARE YOU?

FINE, THANK YOU.

6. FINGERS _____

F	FOUR
	FIVE
	FORK
	FIRST
	FINE
	FINGERS

I HAVE FIVE **FINGERS**.

39. Read and copy the words.

C _____

1. COLOR _____

WHAT COLOR IS THE AMERICAN FLAG?   RED, WHITE, AND BLUE.

2. CAR _____

WHAT **COLOR** IS YOUR **CAR**?   I HAVE A GREEN **CAR**.

3. CARD _____

DO YOU HAVE A SOCIAL SECURITY **CARD**?

YES, I HAVE A SOCIAL SECURITY **CARD**.

SOCIAL SECURITY
532-46-1379
DAVE HAPPY

4. COUNTRY _____

WHAT **COUNTRY** ARE YOU FROM?   I AM FROM THE UNITED STATES.

| **C** | COLOR | CAR | CARD | COUNTRY |

40. Read and copy the words.

_____ **R**

1. DOLLAR _____

HOW MUCH DO YOU HAVE?

I HAVE ONE **DOLLAR.**

2. NUMBER _____

3. LETTER _____

4. FINGER _____

5. COLOR _____

6. SWEATER _____

WHAT **COLOR** IS YOUR **SWEATER?**

PURPLE.

7. ARE _____

HI. HI. HOW **ARE** YOU?

8. CAR _____

9. YOUR _____

WHAT **COLOR** IS YOUR **CAR**? RED.

10. 4 FOUR _____

11. HER _____

HER NAME IS SUE.

_____**R**	NUMBER	LETTER	DOLLAR	ARE	FOUR
YOUR	FINGER	SWEATER	COLOR	CAR	HER

41. Read and copy the words.

N

1. 9 NINE _____

2. NO _____

OH, NO,

3.  NUMBER _____

WHAT IS YOUR TELEPHONE **NUMBER**?

MY TELEPHONE **NUMBER** IS 681-0318,

4. WHAT IS YOUR SOCIAL SECURITY **NUMBER**?

MY SOCIAL SECURITY **NUMBER** IS 532-46-1379,

SOCIAL SECURITY
532-46-1379
DAVE HAPPY
NAME

5. NIGHT _____

6. NAME _____

7. NICE _____

N	NINE NO NUMBER NIGHT NAME NICE

42. Read and copy. **S S S S S S**

S

1. 6 SIX _____

2. 7 SEVEN _____

3. SOCIAL SECURITY _____

WHAT IS HER **SOCIAL SECURITY** NUMBER?

HER **SOCIAL SECURITY** NUMBER IS 982-74-3341.

SOCIAL SECURITY
982-74-3341
MAY LIN
NAME

SP

WHAT DO YOU HAVE?

I HAVE A **SPOON**.

4. SPOON _____

5. SPELL _____

SPELL YOUR FIRST NAME.   S - U - E .

6. SPEAK _____

I **SPEAK** CHINESE.   I **SPEAK SPANISH**.

S	SIX
	SEVEN
	SOCIAL SECURITY

SP	SPOON
	SPELL
	SPEAK
	SPANISH

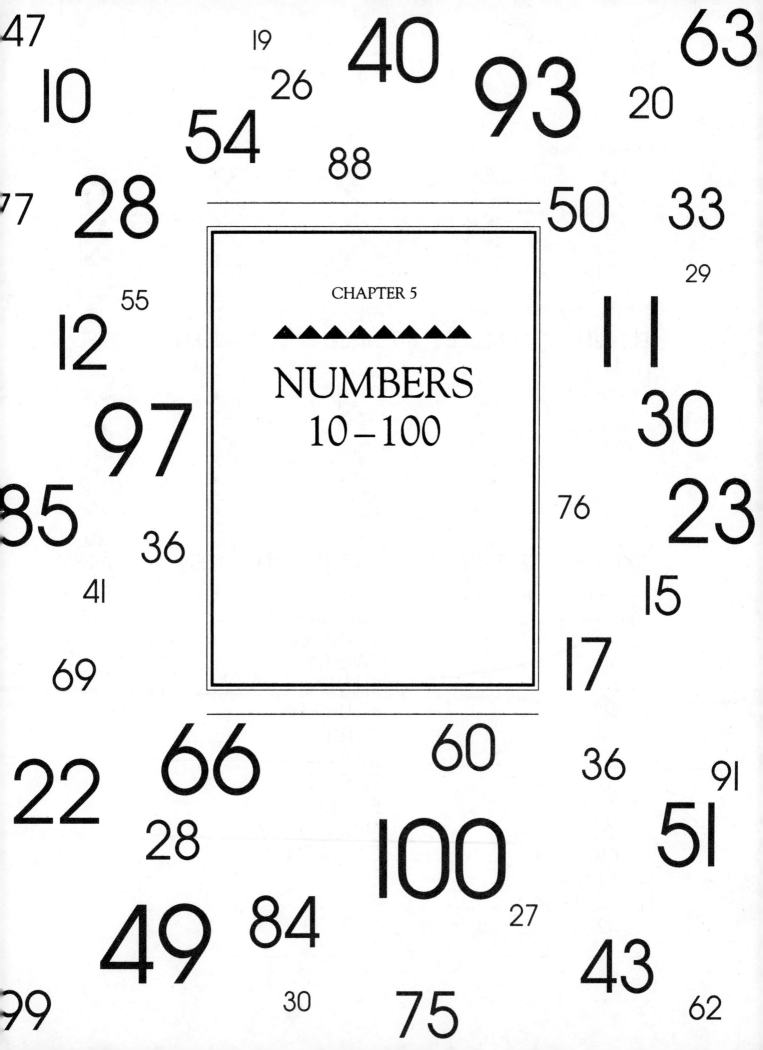

CHAPTER 5

NUMBERS
10 – 100

1. Write the numbers.

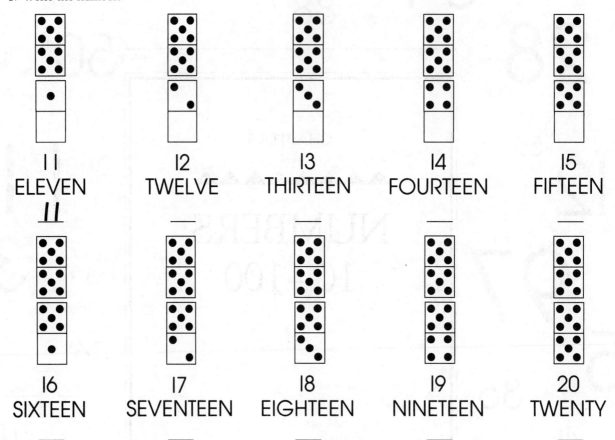

11	12	13	14	15
ELEVEN	TWELVE	THIRTEEN	FOURTEEN	FIFTEEN
11	—	—	—	—

16	17	18	19	20
SIXTEEN	SEVENTEEN	EIGHTEEN	NINETEEN	TWENTY
—	—	—	—	—

2. Draw a line.

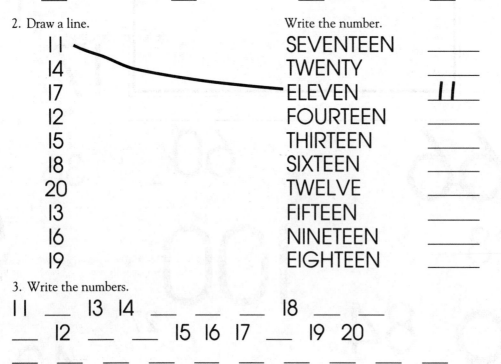

Write the number.

11	SEVENTEEN	___
14	TWENTY	___
17	ELEVEN	*11*
12	FOURTEEN	___
15	THIRTEEN	___
18	SIXTEEN	___
20	TWELVE	___
13	FIFTEEN	___
16	NINETEEN	___
19	EIGHTEEN	___

3. Write the numbers.

11 ___ 13 14 ___ ___ ___ 18 ___ ___

___ 12 ___ ___ 15 16 17 ___ 19 20

___ ___ ___ ___ ___ ___ ___ ___ ___ ___

92

4. Count the dots.

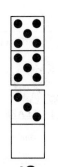 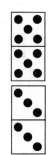 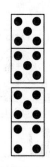 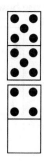

Write the numbers. **13** _____ _____ _____ _____

Print the words. **THIRTEEN** _____ _____ _____ _____

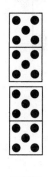  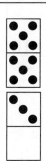 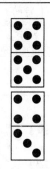 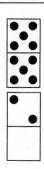 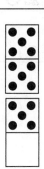

_____ _____ _____ _____ _____

_____ _____ _____ _____ _____

5. Write the numbers and print the words.

17 _____	___ EIGHTEEN	14 _____	___ SEVENTEEN
___ THIRTEEN	11 _____	___ TWENTY	16 _____
19 _____	___ FIFTEEN	12 _____	___ ELEVEN
___ TWELVE	13 _____	___ NINETEEN	20 _____
15 _____	___ SIXTEEN	18 _____	___ FOURTEEN

6. Write the numbers your teacher says (11–20).

   1. **18** ___   2. _____   3. _____   4. _____   5. _____
6. _____   7. _____   8. _____   9. _____   10. _____

7. Write how much.

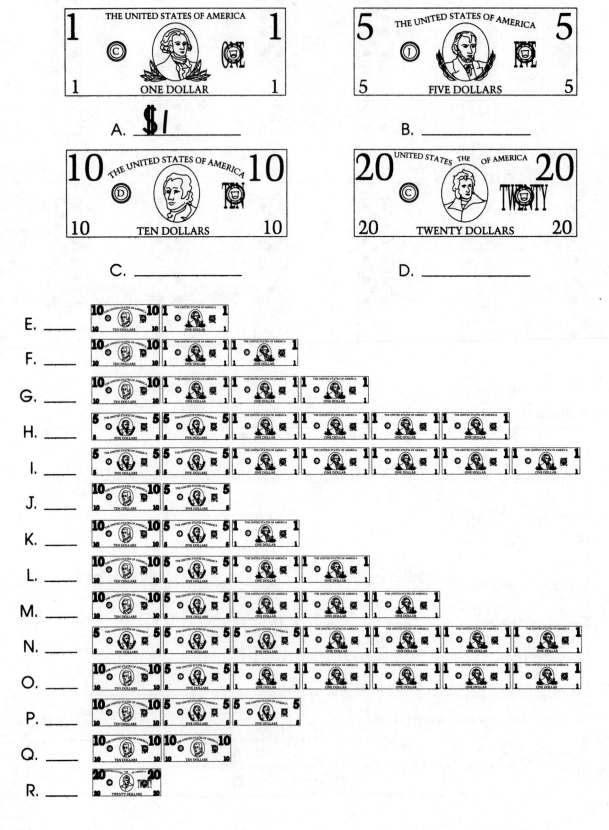

A. __$1__

B. _____

C. _____

D. _____

E. ____

F. ____

G. ____

H. ____

I. ____

J. ____

K. ____

L. ____

M. ____

N. ____

O. ____

P. ____

Q. ____

R. ____

8. Read and copy the words.

1. WINDOW
_ _ _ _ _ _

2. DOOR
_ _ _ _

3. BOOK
_ _ _ _

4. OPEN
_ _ _ _

5. CLOSE
_ _ _ _ _

6. OPEN THE WINDOW.
_ _ _ _ _ _ _ _ _ _ _ _ .

7. CLOSE THE WINDOW.
_ _ _ _ _ _ _ _ _ _ _ _ _ .

8. _ _ _ _ _ THE _ _ _ _ .

9. _ _ _ _ _ YOUR _ _ _ _ .

10. _ _ _ _ _ _ THE _ _ _ _ .

11. _ _ _ _ _ _ YOUR _ _ _ _ .

12. LOCK

13. _ _ _ _ _ _ _ _ _ _ _ _ .

STOP Write the words your teacher says.

14. _____

15. _____

16. _____

17. _____

9. Read.

1. A: (KNOCK, KNOCK)
2. B: COME IN.
3. A: SORRY I'M LATE.
4. B: THAT'S OK.
5. A: NICE TO SEE YOU.
   B: NICE TO SEE YOU.

1.

A

2.

B

3.

A

4.

B

5.

A   B

10. Write the numbers and write the words.

10
TEN
10
TEN

20
TWENTY
__
– – – – – –

30
THIRTY
__
– – – – – –

40
FORTY
__
– – – – – –

50
FIFTY
__
– – – – –

60
SIXTY
__
– – – – –

11. Write the numbers and write the words.

1.

40	30	60	50
FORTY	thirty	SIXTY	fifty
60	50	40	___
sixty	FIFTY	forty	THIRTY

2.

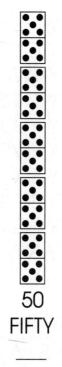

THIRTEEN 13	THIRTY 30
FOURTEEN 14	forty 40
fifteen 15	FIFTY 50
SIXTEEN 16	sixty 60

STOP

12. Write the numbers your teacher says (10, 20, 30, 40, 50, 60, 13, 14, 15, 16).

1. _____   4. _____   7. _____   10. _____

2. _____   5. _____   8. _____   11. _____

3. _____   6. _____   9. _____   12. _____

13. Write the numbers. Draw a line.

____	TWENTY	23
21	TWENTY-ONE	25
____	TWENTY-TWO	20
____	TWENTY-THREE	21
____	TWENTY-FOUR	26
____	TWENTY-FIVE	22
____	TWENTY-SIX	24
____	TWENTY-SEVEN	29
____	TWENTY-EIGHT	28
____	TWENTY-NINE	27

Write the numbers. Draw a line.

____	THIRTY	33
____	THIRTY-ONE	32
____	THIRTY-TWO	30
____	THIRTY-THREE	31
____	THIRTY-FOUR	36
____	THIRTY-FIVE	34
____	THIRTY-SIX	35
____	THIRTY-SEVEN	40
____	THIRTY-EIGHT	39
____	THIRTY-NINE	37
____	FORTY	38

14. Read and copy the numbers.

1	2	3	4	5	6	7	8	9	10
1									
11	12	13	14	15	16	17	18	19	20
21	22	23	24	25	26	27	28	29	30
31	32	33	34	35	36	37	38	39	40

15. Write the numbers.

1	2			5	6			9	
11		13	14			17			20
	22				26		28		
31			34	35				39	

16. Write the number your teacher says (21–40).

1. 24
2. ____
3. ____
4. ____
5. ____
6. ____
7. ____

17. Write the words your teacher says.

8. THIRTY-SEVEN
9. _____
10. _____
11. _____
12. _____
13. _____
14. _____

HOW MUCH IS THIS?

18. Write how much.

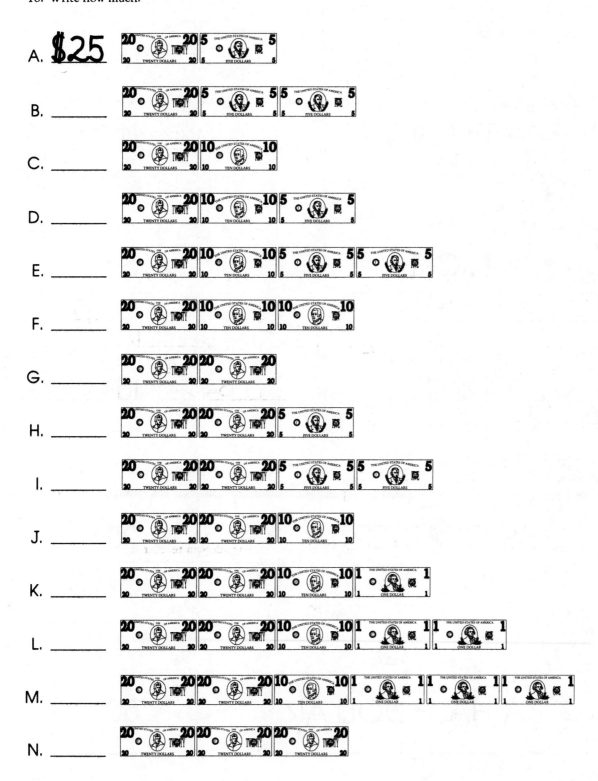

A. $25

B. _____

C. _____

D. _____

E. _____

F. _____

G. _____

H. _____

I. _____

J. _____

K. _____

L. _____

M. _____

N. _____

MONEY

1. _____

19. Read and copy the words.   Write how much.

 A PENNY

2. _ _____

 1¢

3. _____

 A NICKEL

4. _ _____

 5¢

5. _____

 A DIME

6. _ ____

 10¢

7. _____

 A QUARTER

8. _ _____

 25¢

9. _____

 A HALF DOLLAR

10. _ ____ _____

 50¢

11. _____

20. Write how much.

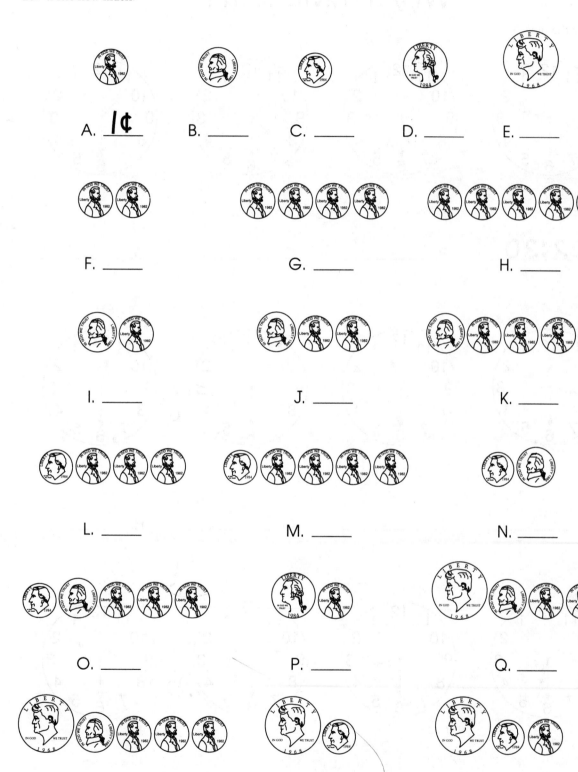

A. __1¢__   B. _____   C. _____   D. _____   E. _____

F. _____   G. _____   H. _____

I. _____   J. _____   K. _____

L. _____   M. _____   N. _____

O. _____   P. _____   Q. _____

R. _____   S. _____   T. _____

WHAT TIME IS IT?

21. Write the time.

A. **2:30**   B. _____   C. _____   D. _____

E. _____   F. _____   G. _____   H. _____

I. _____   J. _____   K. _____   L. _____

22. Draw the time.

A. 5:30   B. 3:30   C. 10:30   D. 1:30

E. 12:30   F. 4:30   G. 9:30   H. 6:30

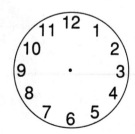  

I. 11:30   J. 2:30   K. 7:30   L. 8:30

23. Read.

1. A: EXCUSE ME.
   B: YES?
   A: WHAT TIME IS IT?
   B: ____ : ____
   A: OH, I'M LATE FOR SCHOOL.

Copy the words.

   1. EXCUSE ME.
   2. _ _ _ _ _ _ _ _.
   3. YES?
   4. _ _ _ ?
   5. WHAT TIME IS IT?
   6. _ _ _ _ _ _ _ _ _ _ _ ?
   7. ____ : ____
   8. OH, I'M LATE FOR SCHOOL.
   9. _ _ , _ _ _ _ _ _ _ _ _ _ _ _ _ _ _.

2. A: EXCUSE ME.
   B: YES?
   A: WHAT TIME IS IT?
   B: ____ : ____
   A: OH, I'M LATE FOR WORK.

   1. EXCUSE ME.
   2. _ _ _ _ _ _ _ _.
   3. YES?
   4. _ _ _ ?
   5. WHAT TIME IS IT?
   6. _ _ _ _ _ _ _ _ _ _ _ ?
   7. ____ : ____
   8. OH, I'M LATE FOR WORK.
   9. _ _ , _ _ _ _ _ _ _ _ _ _ _ _.

104

WHAT TIME IS IT?

24. Write the time.

A. __11:15__ B. __8:45__ C. _____ D. _____

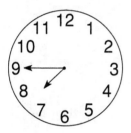

E. _____ F. _____ G. _____ H. _____

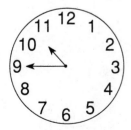

I. _____ J. _____ K. _____ L. _____

25. Draw the time.

 A. 3:45

 B. 10:45

 C. 5:45

D. 9:45

 E. 2:15

 F. 4:15

 G. 10:15

H. 9:15

 I. 5:15

J. 8:15

 K. 4:45

 L. 6:45

26. Write the numbers and write the words.

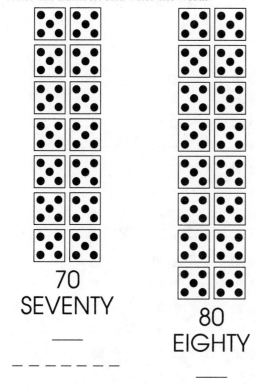

70
SEVENTY

___

_ _ _ _ _ _ _

80
EIGHTY

___

_ _ _ _ _ _

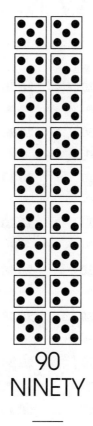

90
NINETY

___

_ _ _ _ _ _

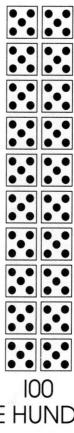

100
ONE HUNDRED

___

_ _ _

_ _ _ _ _ _

27. Listen and repeat.

SEVENTEEN	SEVENTY
17	70
_ _ _ _ _ _ _ _ _	EIGHTY
18	___
NINETEEN	_ _ _ _ _ _
___	90

Write the words and write the numbers.

80	___	70	___
_____	NINETY	_____	ONE HUNDRED
___	100	___	90
SEVENTY	__ _____	EIGHTY	_____

STOP 28. Write the numbers your teacher says. (70, 80, 90, 100, 17, 18, 19)

1. ___ 2. ___ 3. ___ 4. ___ 5. ___ 6. ___ 7. ___ 8. ___ 9. ___ 10. ___

HOW MUCH IS THIS?

29. Write how much.

A. **$70**

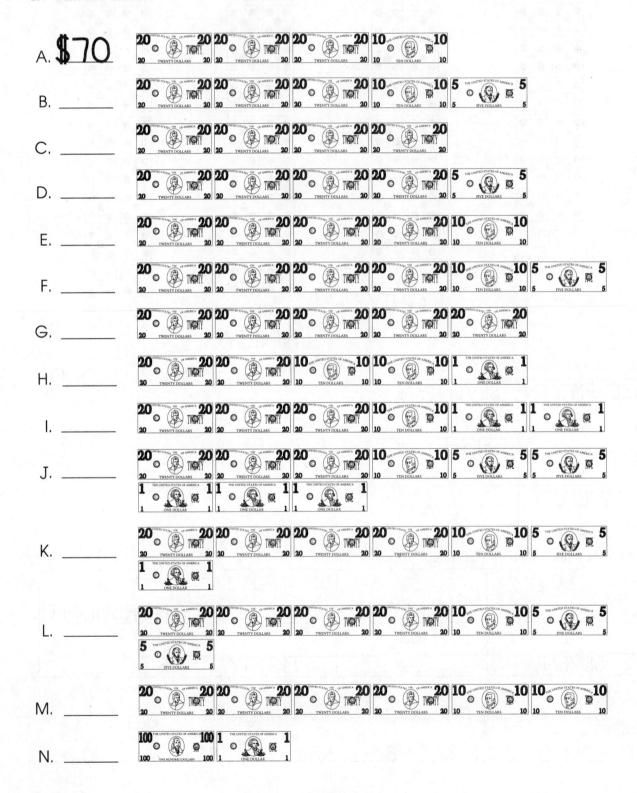

B. _____

C. _____

D. _____

E. _____

F. _____

G. _____

H. _____

I. _____

J. _____

K. _____

L. _____

M. _____

N. _____

30. Write the numbers and write the words.

20 _____	___ EIGHTY	10 ___	___ ONE HUNDRED
___ SIXTY	90 _____	___ SEVENTY	80 _____
40 _____	___ FIFTY	30 _____	___ FORTY
___ TWENTY	100 ___ _____	___ TEN	50 _____
60 _____	___ THIRTY	70 _____	___ NINETY

10 __ __ __ __ __   70 __ __ __

31. Write the numbers.

1			5			9	
	13			17			
22			26				30
		34			38		
			45			49	
				56			
61				67			
	72						80
		83					
			94				100

76 __ __ __   81 __ __ __ __ __   89 __ __

STOP 32. Write the number your teacher says (51–100).

1. 56   2. __   3. __   4. __   5. __   6. __   7. __   8. __

9. __   10. __   11. __   12. __   13. __   14. __   15. __   16. __

33. Read, copy, and answer how old.

AGE

A. _ _ _

HOW OLD IS **SHE**?

B. _ _ _ _ _ _ _ _ _ _ _

12

HOW OLD IS **HE**?

C. _ _ _ _ _ _ _ _ _ _ _ _

63

D.

2

E.

80

F.

14

G.

25

H. I.

J.

36 39 6

K. L.

71 70

N.

M.

O.

4 22 1

P. Q. R.

58 15 20

T. Draw your picture and write your age.

s. HOW OLD ARE **YOU**?

_ _ _ _ _ _ _ _ _ _

110

34. Read and write the year.

1900 1901 _____ 1903 1904 _____ 1906 _____
1908 1909 _____ 1911 1912 _____ _____ 1915
_____ 1917 _____ _____ 1920 1921 _____ 1923
1924 _____ _____ 1927 1928 _____ 1930 1931
1932 _____ _____ 1935 1936 _____ _____ 1939
_____ _____ 1942 1943 _____ _____ 1946 1947
1948 _____ _____ 1951 _____ _____ 1954 _____
_____ _____ _____ 1959 _____ 1961 _____ 1963
_____ _____ 1966 _____ _____ _____ 1970 _____
1972 _____ _____ 1975 _____ _____ 1978 _____
_____ _____ _____ 1983 _____ 1985 _____ 1987
_____ _____ 1990 _____ _____ _____ 1994 _____
1996 _____ 1998 _____ 2000 2001 _____ _____

35. Fill out the form.

NAME _____
          LAST   FIRST   MIDDLE
TELEPHONE NUMBER _____
SOCIAL SECURITY NUMBER _____
COUNTRY _____
LANGUAGE _____
AGE _____

WHAT DAY IS TODAY?

YESTERDAY WAS THURSDAY.

1968

1920

DECEMBER

FEBRUARY

NOVEMBER

WHAT DAY IS TOMORROW?

1952

JANUARY

TUESDAY

1910

CHAPTER 6

▲▲▲▲▲▲▲▲▲

APRIL

MONDAY

THE DATE

MARCH

SUNDAY

JUNE

1976

HAPPY BIRTHDAY!

OCTOBER

JULY

FRIDAY

1945

1990

TODAY IS WEDNESDAY.

WHAT DAY WAS YESTERDAY?

986

WHAT IS THE DATE TODAY?

SEPTEMBER

WHEN IS YOUR BIRTHDAY?

TOMORROW IS SATURDAY.

AUGUST

1. Read and make a check. ☑

A: WHAT **DAY** IS TODAY?

B: TODAY IS
☐ SUN**DAY**.
☐ MON**DAY**.
☐ TUES**DAY**.
☐ WEDNES**DAY**.
☐ THURS**DAY**.
☐ FRI**DAY**.
☐ SATUR**DAY**.

A   B

Copy and write the day today.

1. WHAT **DAY** IS TODAY?

2. _ _ _ _ _ _ _ _ _ _ _ _ _ _ _

3. TO**DAY** IS _____.

4. _ _ _ _ _ _ _ _ _ _____ _

THE DATE

7 DAYS

_ _ _ _ _

2. Draw a line.

TUESDAY   THURSDAY
THURSDAY   MONDAY
FRIDAY   WEDNESDAY
MONDAY   TUESDAY
SATURDAY   SUNDAY
WEDNESDAY   SATURDAY
SUNDAY   FRIDAY

3. Copy the days.

SUNDAY	MONDAY	TUESDAY
_ _ _ _ _ _	_ _ _ _ _ _	_ _ _ _ _ _ _

WEDNESDAY	THURSDAY	FRIDAY	SATURDAY
_ _ _ _ _ _ _ _	_ _ _ _ _ _ _	_ _ _ _ _ _	_ _ _ _ _ _ _

4. Spell the days.

SUNDAY MONDAY TUESDAY WEDNESDAY THURSDAY FRIDAY SATURDAY

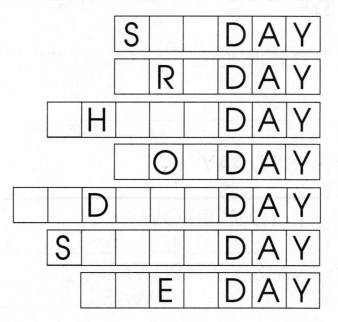

S			D	A	Y

	R		D	A	Y

	H			D	A	Y

	O		D	A	Y

	D			D	A	Y

S				D	A	Y

	E		D	A	Y

115

5. Print the letters.

TODAY
YESTERDAY
TOMORROW
IS
WAS

T						
					I	
Y						

6. Print the days.

SUNDAY   MONDAY   TUESDAY   WEDNESDAY   THURSDAY   FRIDAY   SATURDAY

1. **TODAY** IS _____ .
2. **TOMORROW** IS _____ .
3. **YESTERDAY** WAS _____ .

7. Read and copy the words.

BYE-BYE
SEE YOU TOMORROW.

GOOD-BYE

1. GOOD - BYE .
2. _ _ _ _ - _ _ _ .
3. SEE YOU TOMORROW.
4. _ _ _ _ _ _ _ _ _ _ _ _ _ _

8. Answer the questions.

1. WHAT DAY IS **TODAY**?
   2. T _ _ _ _ IS _____ .
3. WHAT DAY IS **TOMORROW**?
   4. T _ _ _ _ _ _ _ IS _____ .
5. WHAT DAY WAS **YESTERDAY**?
   6. Y _ _ _ _ _ _ _ _ WAS _____ .

9. Copy.

TURN THE LIGHT **ON**. | TURN THE LIGHT **OFF**.

1. ____ ____ ___ **LIGHT** __ __ | 2. ____ ___ ____ ___ _

3. LAMP | 4.

5. TELEVISION | 6. TV

7. RADIO | 8.

Print the words.

9. TURN

10. THE

11. LIGHT

12. LAMP

13. TELEVISION TV

14. RADIO

15. ON

16. OFF

SUNDAY MONDAY TUESDAY WEDNESDAY
THURSDAY FRIDAY SATURDAY

10. Print the letters.

11. Print the days.

1. TODAY IS _____ .

2. TOMORROW IS _____ .

3. YESTERDAY WAS _____ .

12. Fill out the form.

NAME _____
          FIRST   MIDDLE   LAST
COUNTRY _____
LANGUAGE _____
TELEPHONE _____

THE DATE

13. Make an **X** on the words your teacher says.

SATURDAY	THURSDAY	TOMORROW
YESTERDAY	FRIDAY	SUNDAY
TUESDAY	TODAY	IS
WAS	WEDNESDAY	MONDAY

14. Print the words in good English.

1. ? YOU ARE HOW

   HOW ARE YOU ?

2. ? IS TODAY DAY WHAT

   _____ _____ _____ _____ _____

3. WEDNESDAY . TODAY IS

   _____ _____ _____ _____

4. BYE - GOOD

   _____

5. . IS THURSDAY TOMORROW

   _____ _____ _____ _____

6. TOMORROW YOU SEE .

   _____ _____ _____ _____

7. THANK . , FINE YOU

   _____ _____ _____ _____

15. Make a check ☑.

1. TODAY IS ☐   SUNDAY.
           ☐   MONDAY.
           ☐   TUESDAY.
           ☐   WEDNESDAY.
           ☐   THURSDAY.
           ☐   FRIDAY.
           ☐   SATURDAY.

Print the day.

2. TODAY IS _____ .

 the day.

3. WHAT DAY IS TODAY?

SUNDAY MONDAY TUESDAY WEDNESDAY
THURSDAY FRIDAY SATURDAY

4. WHAT DAY WAS YESTERDAY?

SUNDAY MONDAY TUESDAY WEDNESDAY
THURSDAY FRIDAY SATURDAY

5. WHAT DAY IS TOMORROW?

SUNDAY MONDAY TUESDAY WEDNESDAY
THURSDAY FRIDAY SATURDAY

THE DATE

16. Write the numbers.

1. TEN _____
2. TWELVE _____
3. FIFTEEN _____
4. TWENTY-TWO _____
5. FORTY-FOUR _____
6. FIFTY-FIVE _____
7. SEVENTY-SIX _____
8. NINETY-SEVEN _____
9. THIRTY-EIGHT _____
10. SIXTY-THREE _____
11. EIGHTY-ONE _____

17. Write the alphabet.

A _ C _ _ _ _ _ I _ _ _ _
_ O _ _ _ _ _ _ _ _ _ _ _ Z

18. Write the numbers.

10 _ 12 _ _ _ _ _ _ 19 _ _ _
45 _ _ _ _ _ _ _ 53 _ _ _ _
78 _ _ _ _ _ 84 _ _ _ _ _ _

19. Fill out the form.

NAME _____
        LAST   FIRST   MIDDLE

LANGUAGE _____

COUNTRY _____

SOCIAL SECURITY NUMBER _____

PHONE _____

AGE _____

20. Fill in the days (#'s) for this month and this year. Print the month your teacher says.

A CALENDAR

I. _ _ _ _ _ _ _ _ _ _

2. _____ MONTH					3. 19 _____ YEAR	

4. Write the numbers in the boxes.

SUNDAY	MONDAY	TUESDAY	WEDNESDAY	THURSDAY	FRIDAY	SATURDAY

5. WHAT IS THE **DAY** TODAY?

Circle the day. SUNDAY MONDAY TUESDAY WEDNESDAY
THURSDAY FRIDAY SATURDAY

6. PRINT THE DAY.

7. WHAT IS THIS **MONTH**?

Circle the month.

JANUARY	JULY
FEBRUARY	AUGUST
MARCH	SEPTEMBER
APRIL	OCTOBER
MAY	NOVEMBER
JUNE	DECEMBER

8. PRINT THE MONTH.

9. WHAT IS THE **YEAR**? WRITE THE YEAR.

21. Copy the months.

MONTHS	JANUARY	FEBRUARY	MARCH
_ _ _ _ _ _	_ _ _ _ _ _ _	_ _ _ _ _ _ _ _	_ _ _ _ _
	APRIL	MAY	JUNE
	_ _ _ _ _	_ _ _	_ _ _ _

22. Draw a line.

JANUARY   FEBRUARY
JUNE   JANUARY
MARCH   MAY
FEBRUARY   APRIL
MAY   MARCH
APRIL   JUNE

23. Print the letters.

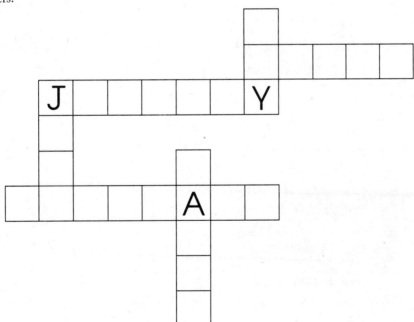

STOP 24. Print the months your teacher says.

1.

2.

3.

4.

5.

6.

25. Read and copy.

HOW IS THE WEATHER?

_ _ _ _ _ _ _ _ _ _ _ _ _ _ _ _ _

1. IT'S SUNNY.
2. IT'S RAINING.
3. IT'S CLOUDY.
4. IT'S WINDY.
5. IT'S FOGGY.
6. IT'S HOT.
7. IT'S COLD.
8. IT'S SNOWING.

1. _____

2. _____

3. _____ 4. _____

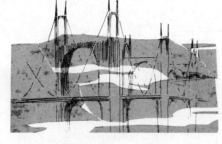

5. _____ 6. _____

7. _____ 8. _____

26. Copy the words.

JULY	AUGUST	SEPTEMBER
_ _ _ _	_ _ _ _ _ _	_ _ _ _ _ _ _ _ _
OCTOBER	NOVEMBER	DECEMBER
_ _ _ _ _ _ _	_ _ _ _ _ _ _ _	_ _ _ _ _ _ _ _

27. Draw a line.

NOVEMBER   JULY

SEPTEMBER   AUGUST

DECEMBER   SEPTEMBER

JULY   OCTOBER

AUGUST   NOVEMBER

OCTOBER   DECEMBER

28. Print the letters.

29. Print the months your teacher says.

1.

2.

3.

4.

5.

6.

THE 12 MONTHS

30. Print the letters.

1. JANUARY
2. FEBRUARY
3. MARCH
4. APRIL
5. MAY
6. JUNE
7. JULY
8. AUGUST
9. SEPTEMBER
10. OCTOBER
11. NOVEMBER
12. DECEMBER

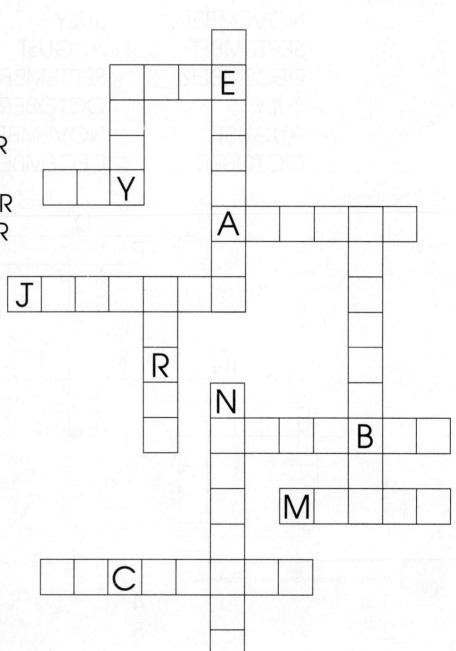

31. Copy.

WHAT **MONTH** IS YOUR BIRTHDAY?

1. _

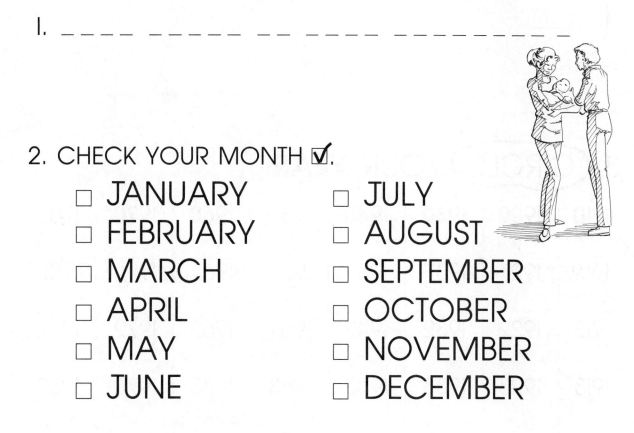

2. CHECK YOUR MONTH ☑.

☐ JANUARY   ☐ JULY
☐ FEBRUARY   ☐ AUGUST
☐ MARCH   ☐ SEPTEMBER
☐ APRIL   ☐ OCTOBER
☐ MAY   ☐ NOVEMBER
☐ JUNE   ☐ DECEMBER

3. PRINT YOUR **MONTH**.

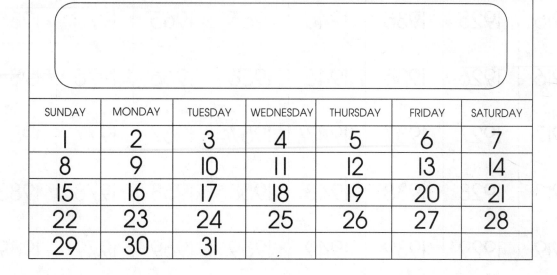

SUNDAY	MONDAY	TUESDAY	WEDNESDAY	THURSDAY	FRIDAY	SATURDAY
1	2	3	4	5	6	7
8	9	10	11	12	13	14
15	16	17	18	19	20	21
22	23	24	25	26	27	28
29	30	31				

32. Copy.

WHAT **YEAR**?

I. _ _ _ _   _ _ _ _   _

Write your year.

2. 19 _ _

3. (CIRCLE) YOUR **YEAR**.

19**10**	19**20**	19**30**	19**40**	19**50**	19**60**	19**70**	19**80**
1911	1921	1931	1941	1951	1961	1971	1981
1912	1922	1932	1942	1952	1962	1972	1982
1913	1923	1933	1943	1953	1963	1973	1983
1914	1924	1934	1944	1954	1964	1974	1984
1915	1925	1935	1945	1955	1965	1975	1985
1916	1926	1936	1946	1956	1966	1976	1986
1917	1927	1937	1947	1957	1967	1977	1987
1918	1928	1938	1948	1958	1968	1978	1988
1919	1929	1939	1949	1959	1969	1979	1989

THE DATE

33. Copy the words.

JANUARY	FEBRUARY	MARCH	APRIL	MAY	JUNE
– – – – – –	– – – – – – – –	– – – – –	– – – – –	– – –	– – – –
JAN.	FEB.	MAR.	APR.		JUN.
– – – .	– – – .	– – – .	– – – .		– – – .

JULY	AUGUST	SEPTEMBER	OCTOBER	NOVEMBER	DECEMBER
– – – –	– – – – – –	– – – – – – – – –	– – – – – – –	– – – – – – –	– – – – – – –
JUL.	AUG.	SEPT.	OCT.	NOV.	DEC.
– – – .	– – – .	– – – – .	– – – .	– – – .	– – – .

34. Draw a line and print the months.

OCTOBER	FEB.	_____
APRIL	JUL.	_____
JULY	MAY	_____
JANUARY	OCT.	**OCTOBER** _____
MAY	AUG.	_____
AUGUST	NOV.	_____
DECEMBER	JUN.	_____
FEBRUARY	APR.	_____
NOVEMBER	DEC.	_____
SEPTEMBER	JAN.	_____
MARCH	SEPT.	_____
JUNE	MAR.	_____

35. Print the abbreviations for the months. (Don't forget the period.)

FEBRUARY	**FEB.** _____	JANUARY	_____
APRIL	_____	MAY	_____
NOVEMBER	_____	AUGUST	_____
SEPTEMBER	_____	DECEMBER	_____
JUNE	_____	JULY	_____
MARCH	_____	OCTOBER	_____

36. Copy the words.

SUNDAY	MONDAY	TUESDAY	WEDNESDAY
_ _ _ _ _ _	_ _ _ _ _ _	_ _ _ _ _ _ _	_ _ _ _ _ _ _ _ _
SUN.	MON.	TUES.	WED.
_ _ _ .	_ _ _ .	_ _ _ _ .	_ _ _ .

THURSDAY	FRIDAY	SATURDAY
_ _ _ _ _ _ _ _	_ _ _ _ _ _	_ _ _ _ _ _ _ _
THURS.	FRI.	SAT.
_ _ _ _ _ .	_ _ _ .	_ _ _ .

37. Draw a line and print the days.

FRIDAY   WED.   _____
MONDAY   FRI.   **FRIDAY** _____
THURSDAY   SUN.   _____
SATURDAY   TUES.   _____
WEDNESDAY   SAT.   _____
SUNDAY   THURS.   _____
TUESDAY   MON.   _____

38. Print the abbreviations for the days. (Don't forget the period.)

SATURDAY   SAT. _____
TUESDAY   _____
FRIDAY   _____
MONDAY   _____
WEDNESDAY   _____
SUNDAY   _____
THURSDAY   _____
SATURDAY   _____

THE DATE

39. Copy the words and numbers.

FIRST	SECOND	THIRD	FOURTH	FIFTH
– – – – – –	– – – – – –	– – – – –	– – – – –	– – – – –
1ST	2ND	3RD	4TH	5TH
– – –	– –	– –	– –	– –

Write the numbers and letters (ST/ ND/ TH).

FIRST   1 ST   FOURTH   _ – –
SECOND   2 – –   THIRD   _ – –
THIRD   3 – –   FIRST   _ – –
FOURTH   4 – –   FIFTH   _ – –
FIFTH   5 – –   SECOND   _ – –

Draw a line.

1ST	THIRD		21ST	TWENTY-THIRD
3RD	FOURTH		23RD	TWENTY-FOURTH
5TH	FIRST		25TH	TWENTY-FIRST
2ND	FIFTH		22ND	TWENTY-FIFTH
4TH	SECOND		24TH	THIRTY-FIRST
			31ST	TWENTY-SECOND

Copy.

TWENTIETH	THIRTIETH
– – – – – – – –	– – – – – – – –
20TH	30TH
– –	– –

131

THE DATE

40. Copy. — — — — — — —

Draw a line.

JAN. 1ST   DECEMBER SECOND
MAY 5TH   AUGUST THIRD
AUG. 3RD   OCTOBER FOURTH
DEC. 2ND   JANUARY FIRST
OCT. 4TH   MAY FIFTH

JUL. 21ST   APRIL THIRTIETH
FEB. 25TH   SEPTEMBER TWENTY-SECOND
APR. 30TH   FEBRUARY TWENTY-FIFTH
MAR. 31ST   NOVEMBER TWENTIETH
NOV. 20TH   JULY TWENTY-FIRST
SEPT. 22ND   JUNE TWENTY-THIRD
JUN. 23RD   MARCH THIRTY-FIRST

41. Write the month and the year. Then write the day numbers in the boxes.

SUNDAY SUN.	MONDAY MON.	TUESDAY TUES.	WEDNESDAY WED.	THURSDAY THURS.	FRIDAY FRI.	SATURDAY SAT.

_____ MONTH   19 __ __ YEAR

42. Make four checks and say the date.

☑
1.

☑
2.

☑
3.

☑
4.

☐ SUN.	☐ JAN.	☐ 1ST	☐ 1989
☐ MON.	☐ FEB.	☐ 2ND	☐ 1990
☐ TUES.	☐ MAR.	☐ 3RD	☐ 1991
☐ WED.	☐ APR.	☐ 4TH	☐ 1992
☐ THURS.	☐ MAY	☐ 5TH	☐ 1993
☐ FRI.	☐ JUN.	☐ 6TH	☐ 1994
☐ SAT.	☐ JUL.	☐ 7TH	☐ 1995
	☐ AUG.	☐ 8TH	☐ 1996
	☐ SEPT.	☐ 9TH	☐ 1997
	☐ OCT.	☐ 10TH	☐ 1998
	☐ NOV.	☐ 11TH	☐ 1999
	☐ DEC.	☐ 12TH	☐ 2000
		☐ 13TH	☐ 2001
		☐ 14TH	☐ 2002
		☐ 15TH	☐ 2003
		☐ 16TH	
		☐ 17TH	
		☐ 18TH	
		☐ 19TH	
		☐ 20TH	
		☐ 21ST	
		☐ 22ND	
		☐ 23RD	
		☐ 24TH	
		☐ 25TH	
		☐ 26TH	
		☐ 27TH	
		☐ 28TH	
		☐ 29TH	
		☐ 30TH	
		☐ 31ST	

WHAT IS THE **DATE** TODAY?

TODAY IS . . .

Write the date.

5. DATE _____ , _____ , _____
DAY   MONTH DAY#   YEAR

43. Read.

JANUARY 1	FEBRUARY 2	MARCH 3	APRIL 4	MAY 5	JUNE 6
JULY 7	AUGUST 8	SEPTEMBER 9	OCTOBER 10	NOVEMBER 11	DECEMBER 12

44. Print the months.

10	11	2
4	9	7
8	6	5
1	12	3

45. Write the date in numbers.

1. JANUARY 8, 1964

   1 - 8 - 64

2. SEPTEMBER 15, 1976

   ___ - ___ - ___

3. DECEMBER 25, 1912

   ___ - ___ - ___

4. FEBRUARY 4, 1945

   ___ - ___ - ___

5. MARCH 23, 1937

   ___ - ___ - ___

6. AUGUST 25, 1920

   ___ - ___ - ___

7. MAY 1, 1937

   ___ - ___ - ___

8. JUNE 27, 1941

   ___ - ___ - ___

9. OCTOBER 14, 1973

   ___ - ___ - ___

10. NOVEMBER 21, 1921

   ___ - ___ - ___

11. JULY 5, 1955

   ___ - ___ - ___

12. APRIL 2, 1923

   ___ - ___ - ___

THE DATE

46. Write the date (Don't forget the comma).

A. 10 - 3 - 80
   OCTOBER 3, 1980

B. 4 - 25 - 71
_____

C. 5 - 13 - 33
_____

D. 6 - 29 - 39
_____

E. 9 - 1 - 29
_____

F. 7 - 21 - 21
_____

G. 8 - 2 - 42
_____

H. 1 - 31 - 64
_____

I. 11 - 19 - 56
_____

J. 2 - 20 - 24
_____

K. 3 - 6 - 75
_____

L. 12 - 30 - 58
_____

47. Write the date.

1. 4 - 21 - 83

2. 3 - 2 - 56

MONTH	DAY	YEAR

MONTH	DAY	YEAR

3. MAY 3, 1974

☐☐ - ☐☐ - ☐☐
MONTH   DAY   YEAR

4. SEPT. 12, 1957

☐☐ - ☐☐ - ☐☐
MONTH   DAY   YEAR

5. JAN. 1, 1965

_____ - _____ - _____
MONTH   DAY   YEAR

6. DATE: (TODAY)

MONTH	DAY	YEAR

7. DATE: (TODAY)

☐☐ - ☐☐ - ☐☐
MONTH   DAY   YEAR

48. Read.

A: WHEN IS YOUR BIRTHDAY?
B: MY BIRTHDAY?
A: YES.
B: JUNE 27TH.
A: OH.

Copy the words.

1. WHEN IS YOUR **BIRTHDAY**?
2. _
3. WRITE YOUR **BIRTHDAY**. _____ _____
                                MONTH   DAY

49. Read.

A: WHAT IS YOUR DATE OF BIRTH?
B: MY BIRTHDATE?
A: YES.
B: JUNE 27TH.
A: WHAT YEAR?
B: 1941.
A: OH. JUNE 27TH, 1941.

Copy.

1. WHAT IS YOUR **DATE OF BIRTH**?
2. _
3. WRITE YOUR **BIRTHDATE**. _____ _____ _____
         MONTH   DAY   YEAR

Copy.

4. WHAT IS THE **DATE** TODAY?
5. _
6. WRITE THE **DATE**. _____ _____ _____
       MONTH   DAY   YEAR

50. Fill out the form.

BIRTHDAY _____ _____
        MONTH   DAY
BIRTHDATE _____ _____ _____
        MONTH   DAY   YEAR
DATE OF BIRTH ☐☐ - ☐☐ - ☐☐
        MONTH   DAY   YEAR
DATE _____ _____ _____
        MONTH   DAY   YEAR

THE DATE

51. Write the days.

SUN.	MON.	TUES.	WED.	THURS.	FRI.	SAT.
				JUNE 1995		
				1	2	3
4	5	6	7	8	9	10
11	12	13	14	15	16	17
18	19	20	21	22	23	24
25	26	27	28	29	30	

1. WHAT **DAY** IS JUNE 1, 1995?
2. THURSDAY
3. WHAT **DAY** IS JUNE 19, 1995?
4. _____
5. WHAT **DAY** IS JUNE 24, 1995?
6. _____

SUN.	MON.	TUES.	WED.	THURS.	FRI.	SAT.
				JUNE 1996		
						1
2	3	4	5	6	7	8
9	10	11	12	13	14	15
16	17	18	19	20	21	22
23 / 30	24	25	26	27	28	29

7. WHAT **DAY** IS JUNE 1, 1996?
8. _____
9. WHAT **DAY** IS JUNE 19, 1996?
10. _____
11. WHAT **DAY** IS JUNE 24, 1996?
12. _____

1999

JANUARY

SUN.	MON.	TUES.	WED.	THURS.	FRI.	SAT.
					1	2
3	4	5	6	7	8	9
10	11	12	13	14	15	16
17	18	19	20	21	22	23
24	25	26	27	28	29	30
31						

FEBRUARY

SUN.	MON.	TUES.	WED.	THURS.	FRI.	SAT.
	1	2	3	4	5	6
7	8	9	10	11	12	13
14	15	16	17	18	19	20
21	22	23	24	25	26	27
28						

MARCH

SUN.	MON.	TUES.	WED.	THURS.	FRI.	SAT.
	1	2	3	4	5	6
7	8	9	10	11	12	13
14	15	16	17	18	19	20
21	22	23	24	25	26	27
28	29	30	31			

APRIL

SUN.	MON.	TUES.	WED.	THURS.	FRI.	SAT.
				1	2	3
4	5	6	7	8	9	10
11	12	13	14	15	16	17
18	19	20	21	22	23	24
25	26	27	28	29	30	

MAY

SUN.	MON.	TUES.	WED.	THURS.	FRI.	SAT.
						1
2	3	4	5	6	7	8
9	10	11	12	13	14	15
16	17	18	19	20	21	22
23	24	25	26	27	28	29
30	31					

JUNE

SUN.	MON.	TUES.	WED.	THURS.	FRI.	SAT.
		1	2	3	4	5
6	7	8	9	10	11	12
13	14	15	16	17	18	19
20	21	22	23	24	25	26
27	28	29	30			

JULY

SUN.	MON.	TUES.	WED.	THURS.	FRI.	SAT.
				1	2	3
4	5	6	7	8	9	10
11	12	13	14	15	16	17
18	19	20	21	22	23	24
25	26	27	28	29	30	31

AUGUST

SUN.	MON.	TUES.	WED.	THURS.	FRI.	SAT.
1	2	3	4	5	6	7
8	9	10	11	12	13	14
15	16	17	18	19	20	21
22	23	24	25	26	27	28
29	30	31				

SEPTEMBER

SUN.	MON.	TUES.	WED.	THURS.	FRI.	SAT.
			1	2	3	4
5	6	7	8	9	10	11
12	13	14	15	16	17	18
19	20	21	22	23	24	25
26	27	28	29	30		

OCTOBER

SUN.	MON.	TUES.	WED.	THURS.	FRI.	SAT.
					1	2
3	4	5	6	7	8	9
10	11	12	13	14	15	16
17	18	19	20	21	22	23
24	25	26	27	28	29	30
31						

NOVEMBER

SUN.	MON.	TUES.	WED.	THURS.	FRI.	SAT.
	1	2	3	4	5	6
7	8	9	10	11	12	13
14	15	16	17	18	19	20
21	22	23	24	25	26	27
28	29	30				

DECEMBER

SUN.	MON.	TUES.	WED.	THURS.	FRI.	SAT.
			1	2	3	4
5	6	7	8	9	10	11
12	13	14	15	16	17	18
19	20	21	22	23	24	25
26	27	28	29	30	31	

13. WHEN IS YOUR BIRTHDAY?

14. _____
       MONTH   DAY

15. CIRCLE YOUR BIRTHDAY ON THE CALENDAR.

16. WHAT DAY IS YOUR BIRTHDAY?

MAKE A CHECK ☑

☐ SUN. ☐ MON. ☐ TUES. ☐ WED.
☐ THURS. ☐ FRI. ☐ SAT.

THE DATE

52. Copy the date.

JANUARY 21, 1965	JAN. 21, 1965	1 - 21 - 65
_ _ _ _ _ _ _ _ _, _ _ _ _	_ _ _. _ _, _ _ _ _	_ - _ _ - _ _

53. Write the date correctly. If OK, print **OK** .

1.	JAN. 21, 65	JAN. 21, 1965
2.	JAN. 21 - 65	
3.	JAN. - 21 - 65	
4.	JANUARY 21, 1965	
5.	JANUARY 21, 1965	OK
6.	JANUARY 21 1965	
7.	JANUARY 21, 65	
8.	JAN. 21, 1965	
9.	JAN 21, 1965	
10.	1 - 21 - 1965	
11.	1 21 65	
12.	1, 21, 65	
13.	1 - 21 - 65	

14. DATE (TODAY) _____

15. DATE OF BIRTH _____

54. Read.

A: HOW OLD ARE YOU?
B: ME?
A: YES.
B: I AM 18 YEARS OLD.

A   B

AGE: 18

Copy the words.

1. HOW OLD IS SHE?
2. _ _ _ _ _ _ _ _ _ _ _ _ _ _ _
Write her age.

3. SHE IS _____ YEARS OLD.
              #
4. _ _ _ _ _ _ _____ _ _ _ _ _ _ _ _ _
                 #
5. AGE: _____
           #

Write your age.

6. HOW OLD ARE YOU?
7. _ _ _ _ _ _ _ _ _ _ _ _ _ _ _
8. I AM _____ YEARS OLD.
          #
9. _ _ _ _____ _ _ _ _ _ _ _ _ _
        #
10. AGE: _____
            #

55. Fill out the form.

NAME _____
        LAST   FIRST   MIDDLE
DATE OF BIRTH _____
COUNTRY _____
PHONE ☐☐☐ - ☐☐☐☐
SOCIAL SECURITY NUMBER ☐☐☐ - ☐☐ - ☐☐☐☐
LANGUAGE _____
AGE _____
DATE _____

56. Read.

A: HOW OLD IS HE?
B: HE IS 34 YEARS OLD.
A: HOW OLD IS SHE?
B: SHE IS 27 YEARS OLD.

A B

AGE: 34

AGE: 27

Copy the words and answer the questions.

1. HOW OLD IS **HE**?
2. _ _ _ _ _ _ _ _ _ _ _ _
3. HE IS 34 YEARS OLD.
4. _ _ _ _ _ _ _ _ _ _ _ _ _ _
5. AGE: _____

I AM
HE IS
SHE IS

6. HOW OLD IS **SHE**?
7. _ _ _ _ _ _ _ _ _ _ _ _
8. SHE IS 27 YEARS OLD.
9. _ _ _ _ _ _ _ _ _ _ _ _ _ _ _ _
10. AGE: _____

11. HOW OLD ARE **YOU**?
12. _ _ _ _ _ _ _ _ _ _ _ _ _
13. I _ _ _____ _ _ _ _ _ _ _ _ _
14. AGE: _____

141

57. Read.

A: HOW OLD ARE THEY?
B: THEY ARE 35 YEARS OLD.
   THEY ARE THE SAME AGE.

HE   SHE
BOB   MARY

AGE: 35   AGE: 35
THEY

Answer the questions.

1. HOW OLD IS HE?
2. HE __ __ ___ YEARS OLD.
   #
3. HOW OLD IS SHE?
4. SHE __ __ ___ YEARS OLD.
   #
5. HOW OLD ARE **THEY**?
6. **THEY** _ _ _ ___ YEARS OLD.
   #
7. THEY ARE THE S_ _ _ AGE.

58. Read and copy.

1.
   WE ARE THE SAME AGE.
   _ _ _ _ _ _ _ _ _ _ _ _ _ _

YOU ARE
WE ARE
THEY ARE

FRANK   SALLY

AGE: 48   AGE: 48

Answer the questions.

2. HOW OLD IS HE?
3. _ _ _ _ ___ YEARS OLD.
   #
4. HOW OLD IS SHE?
5. _ _ _ _ _ ___ YEARS OLD.
   #
6. HOW OLD ARE THEY?
7. _ _ _ _ _ _ ___ YEARS OLD.
   #
8. THEY _ _ _ THE S_ _ _ A_ _ .

142

59. Sing.

THE BIRTHDAY SONG.

Copy.

HAPPY BIRTHDAY TO YOU.

– – – – – – – – – – – – – – – – – –

HAPPY BIRTHDAY TO YOU.

– – – – – – – – – – – – – – – – – –

HAPPY BIRTHDAY DEAR [_____]
FIRST NAME

HAPPY BIRTHDAY TO YOU.

– – – – – – – – – – – – – – – – – –

A: HOW OLD ARE YOU?
   HOW OLD ARE YOU?
B: I AM [__].
        AGE
A: **HAPPY BIRTHDAY** TO YOU.

HAPPY BIRTHDAY TO YOU. HAPPY BIRTHDAY TO YOU.

HAPPY BIRTHDAY, DEAR _____. HAPPY BIRTHDAY TO YOU.

143

WHAT IS HER ADDRESS?

FIFTH AVENUE

THIRD STREET

DO YOU LIVE IN A HOUSE?

FOURTH AVENUE

WHAT CITY DO YOU LIVE IN?

WHAT IS YOUR ZIP CODE?

CHAPTER 7

▲▲▲▲▲▲▲▲

ADDRESSES

BOULEVARD

2043 4TH ST.

GREEN AVENUE

309 5TH AVENUE

WHAT STATE DO YOU LIVE IN?

WHAT IS YOUR APARTMENT NUMBER?

1651 EAST BAY WAY

FIRST STREET

SECOND STREET

DO YOU LIVE IN A FLAT?

HER ADDRESS IS 465 PINE STREET

AVENUE

1. Read, copy, and answer the questions.

A: WHAT **CITY** DO YOU LIVE IN?   A   B

B: I LIVE IN _____.
                          CITY

A: WHAT **STATE** DO YOU LIVE IN?

B: I LIVE IN _____.
                          STATE

1. WHAT **CITY** DO YOU LIVE IN?

2. _ _ _ _ _ _ _ _ _ _ _ _ _ _ _

3. I LIVE IN _____.

4. _ _ _ _ _ _ _ _ _ _ _ _ _ _
                          CITY

5. WHAT **STATE** DO YOU LIVE IN?

6. _ _ _ _ _ _ _ _ _ _ _ _ _ _ _

7. I LIVE IN _____.

8. _ _ _ _ _ _ _ _ _ _ _ _ _ _.
                          STATE

9. I LIVE IN _____ , _____.
                    CITY   STATE

2. Fill out the form.

NAME _____
              LAST   FIRST
PHONE _____
COUNTRY _____
LANGUAGE _____
CITY _____
STATE _____

ADDRESSES

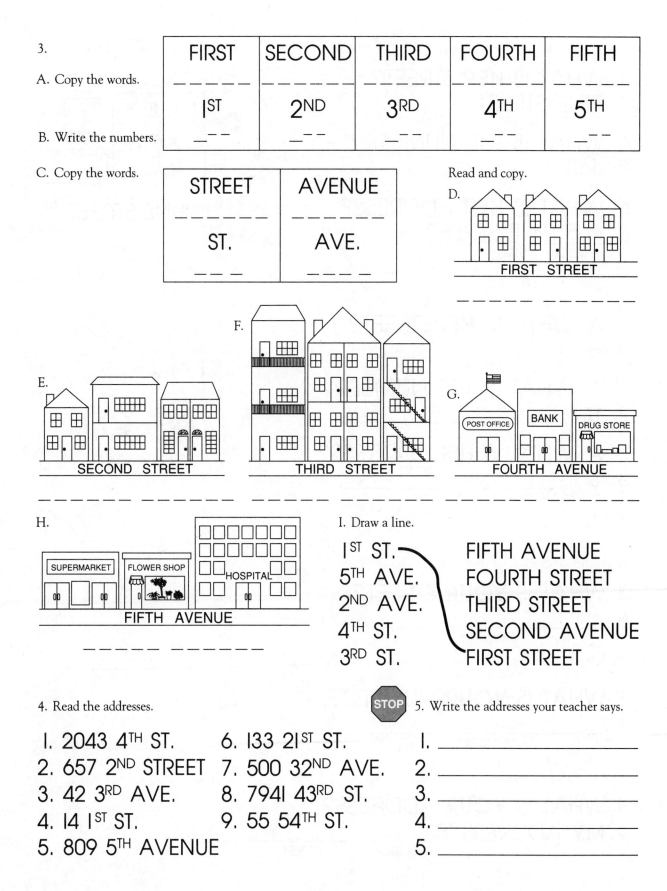

3.

A. Copy the words.

FIRST	SECOND	THIRD	FOURTH	FIFTH
_ _ _ _ _	_ _ _ _ _ _	_ _ _ _ _	_ _ _ _ _ _	_ _ _ _
1ST	2ND	3RD	4TH	5TH

B. Write the numbers.

_ _ _	_ _ _	_ _ _	_ _ _	_ _ _

C. Copy the words.

STREET	AVENUE
_ _ _ _ _ _	_ _ _ _ _ _
ST.	AVE.
_ _ _	_ _ _ _

Read and copy.

D. FIRST STREET

_ _ _ _ _ _ _ _ _ _ _

E. SECOND STREET

F. THIRD STREET

G. FOURTH AVENUE

_ _ _ _ _ _ _ _ _ _ _ _ _ _ _ _ _

H. FIFTH AVENUE

_ _ _ _ _ _ _ _ _ _ _

I. Draw a line.

1ST ST.   FIFTH AVENUE
5TH AVE.   FOURTH STREET
2ND AVE.   THIRD STREET
4TH ST.   SECOND AVENUE
3RD ST.   FIRST STREET

4. Read the addresses.

1. 2043 4TH ST.
2. 657 2ND STREET
3. 42 3RD AVE.
4. 14 1ST ST.
5. 809 5TH AVENUE

6. 133 21ST ST.
7. 500 32ND AVE.
8. 7941 43RD ST.
9. 55 54TH ST.

STOP

5. Write the addresses your teacher says.

1. _____
2. _____
3. _____
4. _____
5. _____

147

6. Read, copy, and answer the questions.

A: WHAT IS **HER** STREET?
B: PINE STREET

A: WHAT IS THE NUMBER?
B: 465

A: WHAT IS **HER** ADDRESS?
B: <u>465 PINE STREET</u>
    NUMBER   STREET

PINE STREET

    A: WHAT IS **HIS** STREET?
1. B: _____

    A: WHAT IS THE NUMBER?
2. B: _____

    A: WHAT IS **HIS** ADDRESS?
3. B: _____
       NUMBER   STREET

FIRST STREET

Answer the questions about your address.

4. WHAT IS **YOUR** STREET?
5. _____
       STREET

6. WHAT IS **YOUR** NUMBER?
7. _____
       NUMBER

8. WHAT IS **YOUR** ADDRESS?
9. **MY** ADDRESS IS _____.
             NUMBER   STREET

7.   ADDRESS
                 1. _ _ _ _ _ _ _

Make a check ✔ if you have this word in your address.   Make a check ✔ if this abbreviation is in your address.

2. ☐ STREET   3. ☐ ST.
   ☐ AVENUE   ☐ AVE.
   ☐ BOULEVARD   ☐ BLVD.
   ☐ DRIVE   ☐ DR.
   ☐ PLACE   ☐ PL.
   ☐ WAY   ☐ WY.
   ☐ _____   ☐ _____

4. ☐ NORTH   5. ☐ N.
   ☐ SOUTH   ☐ S.
   ☐ EAST   ☐ E.
   ☐ WEST   ☐ W.

NORTH
WEST — EAST
SOUTH

Draw a line.   Draw a line.

6. WY.   AVENUE   7. N.   WEST
   ST.   BOULEVARD   E.   SOUTH
   PL.   DRIVE   W.   EAST
   DR.   WAY   S.   NORTH
   BLVD.   PLACE
   AVE.   STREET

8. Write the abbreviations.

1. PLACE   **PL.**   4. WAY   ___   7. NORTH ___
2. DRIVE   ___   5. AVENUE   ___   8. SOUTH ___
3. BOULEVARD ___   6. STREET   ___   9. EAST ___
                                              10. WEST ___

9. Read these addresses.

1. 135 NORTH PINE PLACE   7. 207 THIRD STREET
2. 135 N. PINE PL.   8. 207 3RD ST.
3. 539 WEST TWENTY-FIRST AVENUE   9. 1651 EAST BAY WAY
4. 539 W. 21ST AVE.   10. 1651 E. BAY WY.
5. 84 SOUTH GREEN BOULEVARD   11. 17 SECOND DRIVE
6. 84 S. GREEN BLVD.   12. 17 2ND DR.

10. Read and answer the questions.

1. WHAT **COUNTRY** ARE YOU FROM?

2. I AM FROM _____.
   COUNTRY

3. WHAT **LANGUAGE** DO YOU SPEAK?

4. I SPEAK _____.
   LANGUAGE

5. WHAT IS YOUR **STREET**?

6. _____.
   STREET

7. WHAT IS THE **NUMBER**?

8. _____.
   NUMBER

9. WHAT **CITY** DO YOU LIVE IN?

10. I LIVE IN _____.
    CITY

11. WHAT **STATE** DO YOU LIVE IN?

12. I LIVE IN _____.
    STATE

13. WHAT IS YOUR **ADDRESS**?

14. _____
    NUMBER   STREET

    _____, _____
    CITY   STATE

15. WHAT IS YOUR **NAME**?

16. _____
    FIRST   LAST

11. Read.

Make a check ☑ and write the words.

4. DO YOU LIVE IN AN **APARTMENT**?
5. ☐ YES.   I LIVE IN A_ A_ _ _ _ _ _ _ _.
6. ☐ NO.   I DON'T LIVE IN _N A_ _ _ _ _ _ _ _.

7. DO YOU LIVE IN A **FLAT**?
8. ☐ YES.   I LIVE IN _ F _ _ _.
9. ☐ NO.   I DON'T LIVE IN _ F _ _ _.

10. DO YOU LIVE IN A **HOUSE**?
11. ☐ YES.   I LIVE IN _ H _ _ _ _.
12. ☐ NO.   I DON'T LIVE IN _ H _ _ _ _.

13. WHAT IS YOUR **APARTMENT NUMBER**?
14. ☐ MY **APARTMENT** IS # _ _ _ _ _ _ _ _ .
15. ☐ NO APARTMENT #.
16. ADDRESS _____
         NUMBER   STREET   APT. #

         _____, _____
         CITY   STATE

12. Read, copy, and write your zip code.

A: WHAT IS YOUR **ZIP CODE**?
B: MY ZIP CODE IS 94133.

1. WHAT IS YOUR ZIP CODE?
2. _____ __ ____ ___ ____?
3. MY ZIP CODE IS ☐☐☐☐☐.

13. Print the letters.

ADDRESS
NUMBER
STREET
APARTMENT
CITY
STATE
ZIP CODE

Z D
A T
Y
M
S T
S

14. Write your address.

ADDRESS

NUMBER _____
STREET _____
APARTMENT # _____
CITY _____
STATE _____
ZIP CODE _____

ADDRESSES

15. Copy.

ADDRESS

I. _ _ _ _ _ _ _

Print your address.

2.

| | | | | | | | | | | | | | | | | | | | | | |
NUMBER   STREET   APT. #

3.

| | | | | | | | | | | | | | | | , | | | | | | | | |
CITY   STATE   ZIP CODE

4. ADDRESS _____
NUMBER   STREET   APT. #

5. _____ , ____ _____
CITY   STATE   ZIP CODE

16. Print your name and address on the envelope.

_____
NAME

_____
NUMBER   STREET   APT. #

_____
CITY   STATE   ZIP CODE

USA ¢

153

17. Read the addresses.

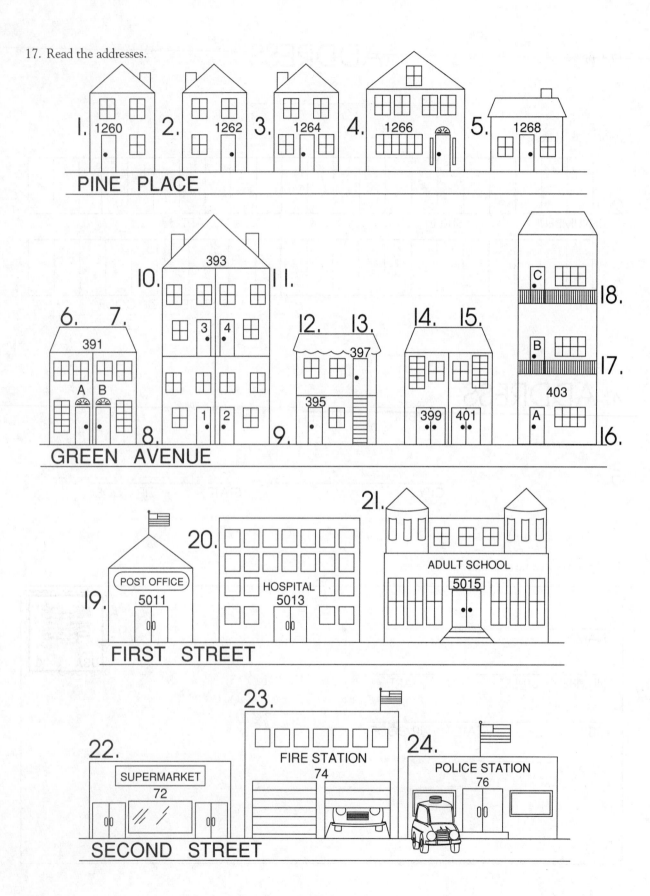

1. 1260
2. 1262
3. 1264
4. 1266
5. 1268

PINE PLACE

6. 7. 391 A B
8.
9.
10. 393 3 4 1 2
11.
12. 395
13. 397
14. 399
15. 401
16. A 403
17. B
18. C

GREEN AVENUE

19. POST OFFICE 5011
20. HOSPITAL 5013
21. ADULT SCHOOL 5015

FIRST STREET

22. SUPERMARKET 72
23. FIRE STATION 74
24. POLICE STATION 76

SECOND STREET

ADDRESSES

18. Fill out the form.

NAME _____
           LAST   FIRST   MIDDLE

ADDRESS _____
          NUMBER   STREET   APT. #

_____, _____
    CITY   STATE   ZIP CODE

TELEPHONE _____

SOC. SEC. NUMBER _____

BIRTHDATE _____
         MONTH   DAY   YEAR

AGE _____

COUNTRY _____

LANGUAGE _____

DATE _____

19. Read and copy the words.

W

1. WHAT _____

2. WEST _____

WHAT IS YOUR ADDRESS?

25 **W.** PINE STREET APT. #201.

NORTH
WEST — EAST
SOUTH

3. WHITE _____

WHAT COLOR IS THE AMERICAN FLAG?

RED, **WHITE**, AND BLUE.

4. WEATHER _____

5. WINDY _____

HOW IS THE **WEATHER**?

IT'S **WINDY** TODAY.

6. WHERE --

WHERE IS THE POST OFFICE? OVER THERE.

7. WATCH --

WHAT TIME IS IT? I DON'T KNOW. I DON'T HAVE A WATCH.

8. WE --

WE ARE THE SAME AGE.

YESTERDAY WAS WEDNESDAY.

TODAY IS THURSDAY.

SUN.	MON.	TUES.	WED.	THURS.	FRI.	SAT.
	1	2	3	4	5	6
7	8	9	10	11	12	13
14	15	16	17	18	19	20
21	22	23	24	25	26	27
28	29	30	31			

9. WAS --

10. WEDNESDAY --

W	WHAT	WEST	WHITE	WEATHER
	WINDY	WHERE	WATCH	WE WAS
	WEDNESDAY			

20. Read and copy the words.

C

1. COLD

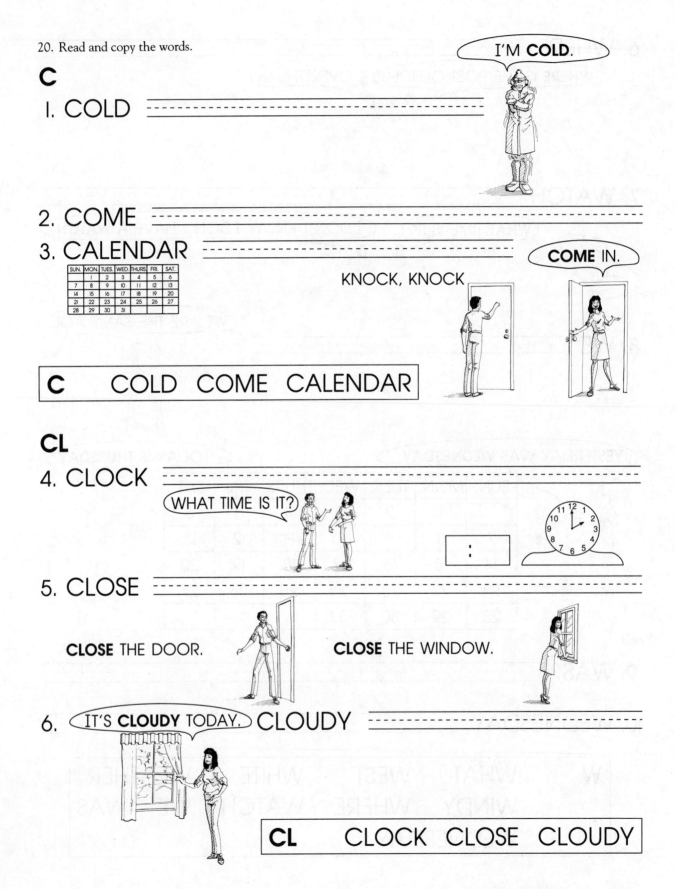

I'M **COLD**.

2. COME

3. CALENDAR

SUN.	MON.	TUES.	WED.	THURS.	FRI.	SAT.
	1	2	3	4	5	6
7	8	9	10	11	12	13
14	15	16	17	18	19	20
21	22	23	24	25	26	27
28	29	30	31			

KNOCK, KNOCK

COME IN.

C COLD COME CALENDAR

CL

4. CLOCK

WHAT TIME IS IT?

5. CLOSE

CLOSE THE DOOR.

CLOSE THE WINDOW.

6. IT'S **CLOUDY** TODAY. CLOUDY

CL CLOCK CLOSE CLOUDY

21. Read and write PUSH or PULL.

1. _ _ _ _

2. _ _ _ _

3. _ _ _ _

4. _ _ _ _

PUSH
PULL

5. _ _ _ _

6. _ _ _ _

7. _ _ _ _

8. _ _ _ _ OUT

22. Read and copy the words.

P

1. PUSH -

PUSH THE DOOR.   **PUSH** THE CART.

2. PULL -

PULL THE DOOR.   **PULL** HIS TOOTH OUT.

3. PEN -

I HAVE A BLACK **PEN.**

4. PENCIL -

I HAVE TWO **PENCILS.**

160

5. PENNY

A **PENNY** IS I¢.

6. POST OFFICE

THE **POST OFFICE** IS OVER THERE.

POST OFFICE

7. POLICE

A **POLICE** CAR IS OVER THERE.

POLICE STATION 26

| P | PUSH PULL PEN PENCIL PENNY POST OFFICE POLICE |

23. Read and copy the words.

_____**CK**

1. LOCK _____

LOCK THE DOOR.

2. KNOCK KNOCK _____

3. BLACK _____

4. JACKET _____

MY **JACKET** IS **BLACK**.

5. CLOCK _____

WHAT TIME IS IT?

:

_____**K**

6. THANK

COME IN.   **THANK** YOU.

7. PINK

I HAVE A **PINK** SWEATER.

8. WORK

I'M LATE FOR **WORK**.

9. FORK

CK	LOCK	KNOCK	BLACK	CLOCK	JACKET
K	THANK	PINK	WORK	FORK	

24. Read and copy the words.

IT'S **SUNNY** TODAY.

S

1. SUNNY

2. SEPTEMBER

SUNDAY	MONDAY	TUESDAY	WEDNESDAY	THURSDAY	FRIDAY	SATURDAY
1	(2)	3	4	5	6	7
8	9	10	11	12	13	14
15	16	17	18	19	20	21
22	23	24	25	26	27	28
29	30					

3. SECOND

4. SUNDAY

5. SATURDAY

6. SIXTY

HE IS **60** YEARS OLD.

7. SEVENTY

8. SORRY

9. SUPERMARKET

10. SEE

S	SUNNY	SEPTEMBER	SECOND	SUNDAY	SATURDAY
	SIXTY	SEVENTY	SORRY	SUPERMARKET	SEE

Alphabet and Number Reference Guide

PRINT.

A B C D E F G H I J K L M
N O P Q R S T U V W X Y Z

print.

a b c d e f g h i j k l m
n o p q r s t u v w x y z

Write.

Aa Bb Cc Dd Ee Ff
Gg Hh Ii Jj Kk Ll
Mm Nn Oo Pp Qq Rr
Ss Tt Uu Vv Ww Xx
Yy Zz

NUMBERS.

1 2 3 4 5 6 7 8 9 10